The Analysis of Music

The Analysis of Music

Second Edition

JOHN D. WHITE

The Scarecrow Press, Inc.
Metuchen, N.J., and London. 1984

First edition published by Prentice-Hall, Inc., 1976.

Library of Congress Cataloging in Publication Data

White, John David, 1931-
   The analysis of music.

   Includes bibliographical references and index.
   1. Musical analysis. I. Title.
MT6.W4147A6   1984   780'.1'5   84-5437
ISBN 0-8108-1701-2

Contents

iii

102489

7

Counterpoint,   127

8

The Element of Sound,   160

9

An Approach to Musical Sound in Analysis,   182

10

Synthesis and Conclusions,   204

Index,   210

Author's Foreword

The Analysis of Music was first published almost a decade ago by Prentice-Hall. At that time the point of view I was presenting needed advocacy, and I still think it does—namely that meaningful musical analysis must deal with all of the elements of music in such a way as to show that musical style, meaning, and design are the results of the combined forces of melody, harmony, rhythm, and sound rather than by factors of pitch alone. While the validity of that stance seems obvious, it is a point of view that has not been universally honored by present-day theorists, some of whom seem to have adopted narrow analytical approaches to the exclusion of an integrated approach. The result often is that the factors which lend meaning to musical sound in a particular context are obscured in order to follow blindly a particular academic technique whether or not it is appropriate to a given situation. Their approaches are valid in themselves. It is not the techniques but the occasional obsessive and unmusical attitudes which cause the abuses.

This, in part, may be related to the fact that theoretical study has never before been given as much attention as it is today. For it is now recognized as a vital component of every musician's training and in many instances is being taught better than ever before. But the sad fact is that—though we theorists may rightly call ourselves scholars—not all of us are sufficiently involved as *musicians* to qualify for the task of assessing music through analysis. This is apparent in our teaching, and the unfortunate result is that, even in some of our finest institutions of higher learning, music majors still regard the sequence of theory courses as needless hurdles—obstacles to be surmounted so that they can get on with their real business of music making. The blame, in my opinion, must rest directly upon the shoulders of theory teachers who tend to sterilize music, who seem to view the analytical task as a clinical or surgical procedure unrelated to musical performance and composition. Some such theorists are visible in our scholarly associations and publish in our journals. In the academic world one does this, of course, and I am a dutiful and sometimes enthusiastic member of our theoretical associations. But occasionally the written product of such activity communicates the message that some theorists are unfamiliar with vast areas of our concert repertoire, and are unconcerned with music making as it is practiced in the best performance and composition studios.

Examples in point are the scholar who writes that "melody is any collection of pitches," ignoring the importance of the factors of rhythm and sound; one who rhapsodizes over an harmonic phenomenon in Mozart while revealing that he is totally unaware of the ubiquity and significance of that phenomenon in music before, during, and after Mozart; and those who analyze the music of Webern from a set-theoretical perspective without considering the overwhelming significance of timbre, texture, dynamics, and rhythm in the very works being analyzed.

Such blunders reveal a lack of the kind of musical understanding that is normally acquired through years of music making. There are, after all, only two kinds of musicians—those who write music and those who play it. The ideal theorist is one who has done a great deal of both, is well versed in music history, and who possesses specialized theoretical skills. Theorists tend to zero in on particular techniques which in themselves are marvelous tools for analysis; but these same tools can obscure the real meaning of music if the analyst is blinded by the process. (Schenkerian analysis and set theory both possess the unfortunate feature of tending to obscure the significance of real pitch over pitch-class and the importance of rhythmic articulation in macro-structure.) The theorist must rely upon his innate and acquired musicality to be sure that his observations are based upon the real experience of music rather than upon fascination with an analytical process. This, then, is an exhortation for theorists to renew their ties to the world of music making, and to communicate by example to their students that music analysis does not exist in a vacuum.

Indeed, analysis is the *sine qua non* of every musician's task. As I have said elsewhere,* the finest artists use analysis constantly in rehearsal and performance whether they are aware of it or not. The studio performance professor who teaches *music* (and not just technique) must be aware of this, if only subconsciously; for even at the beginning levels of music performance, no technical problem can be approached without musical insights revealed by analysis. Technique and musical analysis enjoy a symbiotic relationship of the highest order. For the theory sequence to be truly meaningful to performance and composition students, this relationship must be seen as a way of life in the theory classroom.

Guidelines for College Teaching of Music Theory by John D. White (Metuchen, N.J.; Scarecrow Press, 1981) pp. 118-119.

A major objective of *The Analysis of Music* was to do just that in the form and analysis class. In this second edition of the book, aside from correcting errors and misconceptions, I have added an elementary section on sets and interval vectors which I hope will be used judiciously; and I have added a new Chapter Nine entitled "An Approach to Musical Sound in Analysis." Except for such additions and changes, most of the book remains as it was when it first appeared in 1975. Thus, it retains whatever virtues it had then, and I have tried to eliminate its faults. I am indebted to a number of colleagues and students who have identified errors or called my attention to ways in which the book could be improved. Among these is Professor Reid Poole of University of Florida whose perceptive comments were most helpful, and who also invited me to meet with his Form and Analysis Class to discuss the revision of this book. These talented undergraduates presented numerous student reactions, many of which have been incorporated into this Second Edition. I also thank Janeen Larsen, a University of Florida graduate student, who called my attention to a flagrant error. I believe that the book is now better than the First Edition, and hope that it will be found to be relevant and challenging to students of musical analysis.

JOHN D. WHITE
University of Florida

Preface to the First Edition

In a recent issue of the *Journal of Music Theory* the first paragraph of an excellent article on musical structure ended with the sentence, "There is still no textbook in which pedagogically satisfactory techniques of analysis are presented." It is surprising, considering the wealth of literature on musical form and style, that there are not several analytical method texts for students of performance, composition, and musicology. Although there are many fine books on form, and a few on style, there remains a great need for a real "how to" book for the student of musical analysis. *The Analysis of Music* attempts to fill that need.

The book is designed for use in the general music analysis course usually required of music students during their junior year. Although it presupposes a two-year background in music theory, I believe that it could also be used in the sophomore theory course.

Its purpose is to outline a basic system or plan for analysis, and to carry the student through many aspects of the analytical process using examples of music from the Middle Ages to the twentieth century. The traditional approach to the study of musical form involves the use of formal stereotypes as measuring sticks of exceptional practices in actual examples of these forms. As present-day theorists have become increasingly conscious of the fact that these so-called exceptional practices are the prime elements of stylistic individuality, the "forms" themselves have been relegated to a less significant position and greater attention has been given to musical style. Nevertheless, the analysis of form is a part of style analysis, and the traditional taxonomy of forms—binary, rondo, sonata form, etc.—still serves a purpose at the descriptive stage of analysis. The title of Chapter 4 (Normative Structures) is a clue to the fact that I treat these forms for what I believe they are—skeletal outlines based upon normative practices of the past to which live pieces of music often bear superficial resemblances.

xi

Chapters 5 through 8 deal with the elements of music. In these chapters specific musical examples are used to show the relationship of these elements to the total form and style of the music. Chapter 8 deals in depth with the elements of texture and dynamics in relation to form and style, a treatment often neglected in the study of musical analysis. Tone color or timbre, too long the exclusive domain of the orchestration course, is also covered in this chapter. Chapter 9* contains further discussion of the growth process and sets the example for drawing value judgments and other meaningful conclusions about musical works.

Students of analysis learn partly by precept but most of all by example. Brief illustrations of various aspects of analysis are sprinkled throughout the book. These include short excerpts, large sections, and complete movements. Once the analytical method begins to take shape, students will profit from specific assignments of complete works from various periods in music history.

At the risk of being idiosyncratic, I have introduced a few self-coined terms for use in analysis. Most of these are obvious and simple such as 0 for organic unity and the choices of R, D, V, or N in the growth process (repetition, development, variation, or new material). The CT factor (repose/tension) may be a bit more obscure, although it should become increasingly understandable as it is used in the course of the book.

A number of people have contributed to the preparation of the book. Norwell Therien, Jr., Prentice-Hall's music editor, and Jamie Fuller, production editor, were helpful through their patience and good counsel. I am also indebted to the cumulative influence of many fine musical colleagues and students with whom I have been associated over the years, and to David and Michele, who helped with the index. But for the book's shortcomings I alone am responsible. I will be pleased if it contributes in any way to the understanding of musical style, for that is the purpose not only of the book, but also of the study of music theory.

JOHN D. WHITE

---

*Chapter 10 in the Second Edition.

The Analysis of Music

1

The Purpose and Nature
of Analysis

The study of music theory has long been considered one of the most important features of a musician's training. Its essential purpose—aside from sight-singing, score reading, and other important performance skills—is the understanding of musical style. Indeed, from the time in his training when a musician first acquires sufficient technique to creditably perform a piece of music, he begins to learn about style; for in the preparation of any work for performance, he must be guided by his own stylistic judgments. A certain manner of bowing may be appropriate to a Bartók violin passage; degrees of accelerando or ritard may be controlled by factors such as harmonic rhythm, density, length of the work, or historical performance practices; a subtle rhythmic inflection may bring out the true beauty of a modulation in a Schubert trio; a harpsichordist may find reason to alter the texture of the figured-bass realization in a Corelli trio sonata; a woodwind player selects or makes a certain kind of reed for a certain kind of music; a singer uses portamenti very sparingly in the music of one composer, but not of another; a conductor asks for dotted rhythms in a baroque work to be played in a certain stylized way—the list could go on endlessly. These are the kinds of discriminative judgments that may become almost second nature to fine performers. And they are all in the realm of musical style.

One of the chief purposes of musical analysis, if not the essential purpose, is to give the musician a systematic method with which to approach questions of musical style. Comprehension of stylistic differences between the music of two composers, or between two periods or movements in music history, is as important to the performer as it is to the composer or musicologist. Whether a fine violinist's understanding and knowledge of style is acquired painstakingly through years of study, or instinctively through listening and performing, he consciously makes stylistic judgments and distinctions which are of vital importance to the excellence and beauty of his

1

performances. His knowledge of style demands that he play the Mozart G Major Concerto with a different kind of technique from that used for the Sibelius Concerto. His understanding of Mozart's style may result in his fingering a passage a certain way, and his manner of bowing certain passages in the Sibelius may be governed, consciously or not, by what he knows about the style of that piece of music and that composer. This is why the greatest performers are intelligent artists who approach each piece of music thoughtfully on its own stylistic terms, bringing all of their insights to bear on the problems of interpretation. And this is why, having once acquired technical competence on an instrument, the performer more often than not confronts problems which are basically musical rather than technical. At a superficial level the fingering of a fugue from *The Well-Tempered Clavier* may appear to be a technical problem, but at a deeper level it demands a musical and stylistic approach, for the pianist must determine the appropriate articulation, and hence, the manner of fingering, from his knowledge of Bach's style.

Another who must make distinctions and judgments based on his knowledge of musical style is the composer. It is simple but profoundly true that the music of every composer is the end product of all the music that he knows, distilled and renewed by his own creativity. The more thoroughly he understands the musical styles of the past, the more capable he is of finding uniquely expressive points of departure (innovations, if you will) from those styles into the fresh new world of his own music. The composer, of course, profits doubly from the study of musical style because in dealing with the styles of the past he comes to grips with the techniques of manipulating musical tones. In studying an invention or fugue of Bach he learns contrapuntal techniques and begins to practice, as it were, the techniques of musical composition.

The historian, critic, or musicologist also relies heavily upon his knowledge of musical style, for the value judgments that he is called upon to make in journals and books must be based upon a thorough knowledge of musical styles throughout history. Indeed, for the musicologist—the scientist and philosopher of music—analysis of musical style is the prime task. Whether applied to a single work, the total output of a composer, or a certain genre of music, style analysis is the basic tool leading to comparisons, distinctions, judgments, and finally to enlightening conclusions about music—its creation, its existence, and its performance.

STYLISTIC NORMS

Whether aiming at practical performance or the other extreme of abstract musical speculation, there has always been the danger that a theoretical system might dominate the user at the expense of genuine musical understanding or creativity. A musician studying the Bach chorales may discover that a certain standard harmonic progression (such as that shown in Figure 1) occurs frequently and almost always in the same relationships to

Figure 1

phrase, melody, and rhythm. This defines a norm, but if he views this norm simply as a rule of composition, or as an example to be followed in the construction of harmonic exercises, he is artificially dominated by a rule established after the fact of the music itself. If, however, the musician interprets the norm as a point of departure in the composition or analysis of music, or as knowledge to be used in the interpretation of music, then he is using his newly acquired knowledge to enhance his musical understanding.

Debussy said, "Rules are created by works of art, not for works of art." This can be interpreted to mean that, although certain characteristic musical phenomena may occur in a composer's works often enough to suggest "rules" or norms, such normative phenomena, if applied strictly by another composer, probably would result not in a fine work of art but in a lifeless imitation of a style. Of course, a composer may use practices of other composers as points of departure, but ideally his departures from the norms of a period or school of composition create fresh musical effects. The use of established musical techniques and devices identifies a composer in terms of his relationships to his contemporaries, predecessors, historical period, school or movement; while the composer's creative departures from these norms define his own unique musical style. The fact that composers usually start from a foundation of pre-existing techniques and practices makes it possible for the analyst to use this foundation of normative musical phenomena as a point of departure to show what is strikingly fresh and new in a given composer's music.

The so-called common practice of the eighteenth and early nineteenth centuries functions as a set of very useful norms in the analysis of eighteenth- nineteenth- and even twentieth-century music. It is assumed that the beginning student of style analysis will be well acquainted with music written during the common practice period when the diatonic tonal system was at its height. Some knowledge of the music of earlier periods, particularly that of the Renaissance and early baroque periods, will also be useful. During the eighteenth century and well into the romantic period, four-part vocal writing and thorough bass were considered the prime ingredients for the beginning study of musical composition. Thorough bass, the baroque shorthand technique of notating and interpreting figured bass either on paper or in performance, is most useful as a means of describing or symbolizing harmonic passages in homophonic music.

The first courses in music theory are often concerned almost entirely with the normative harmonic and contrapuntal practices of the eighteenth and early nineteenth centuries. Ideally, the purpose of that study is not to learn how to create sterile imitations of a style, but to establish a frame of reference—to learn these normative musical phenomena to use as points of departure in beginning attempts at style analysis. It is true, of course, that the exercises produced in order to learn the style of the common practice period do not really represent the style of any music composed at that time, for each composer's departures from the norm define his own unique style. Just as the statistical "average person" does not really exist, so the normative musical phenomena of the common practice period, if synthesized, produce a style that does not exist. But this non-existent style is nevertheless very useful in the description and analysis of music. And, as stated earlier, the prime purpose of the study of music theory (aside from sight-singing and other reading and performance skills) is to analyze musical style and to use the knowledge gleaned from this analysis in one of the musical disciplines— performance, composition, or musicology. To do this the student will need the knowledge normally acquired in the beginning study of music theory. But he will also need the concepts and terminology gained from the study of music history and literature as well as the knowledge and perceptions necessary to musical performance. All of these play a part in meaningful style analysis.

THE NATURE OF ANALYSIS

At the outset it is easier to say what analysis is not than to say what it is. We can show some of the things it isn't by examining the familiar example in Figure 2. The chordal pattern appears to form a progression of a major-minor seventh chord with C as root, an F major triad, a major-minor seventh chord with G as root, an A minor triad, a major-minor seventh chord with D as root, and a G major triad. We have noted that much about the progression, but is this analysis? No, it is merely observation, for we have not shown any relationship between the sonorities, we have not shown how the music proceeds in time from one moment to the next, we have said nothing about a larger time-span—how it contributes to what will follow—nor have we related the excerpt to the general style of the composer or the time in history when it was composed. Indeed, such a simplistic harmonic description can obscure the real harmonic significance of the passage. The analyst may begin with such observations, but they serve only as points of departure.

Adagio molto

Figure 2: Beethoven, Symphony No. 1, Introduction

The analyst will be proceeding in the right direction if he notes that the passage can be described harmonically within the key of C major as V^7/IV–IV–V^7–VI–V^7/V–V. This too, taken by itself, can be misleading. By relating the progression to a tonic and assigning names and numbers within the key of C major we have begun the analytical process with a meaningful observation. But a description of this sort is a tool for analysis, not its end purpose. Observation or description frequently masquerades as analysis—in studies tabulating the frequency of certain sonorities in a piece of music or a body of works, in twelve-tone studies which do little more than find all the forms and transpositions of the row, or in notes on record jackets or concert programs. Information secured by set analysis and vector analysis of intervals can be used for description and observation (and can be processed by computer) provided that the analyst is highly selective of his data. The analyst must always bear in mind, however, that unless he uses his information to draw meaningful conclusions about musical style, he is missing the point of analysis.

Having described the passage in Figure 2 with Roman numerals within a key, the analyst is once again back at the stage of observation and description. Using his listening ability and his perception of tonic-dominant relationships, he should now note that the key center is deliberately obscured until the end of the passage. He should describe Beethoven's method of doing this and begin to speculate upon its artistic rationale. This will require examination of the full score and will open the door to observations about phenomena other than the harmonic element—rhythmic structure, orchestration, texture, motivic relationships, etc. His ultimate goal is to draw conclusions about Beethoven's style and the style of the first symphony which will be useful in performing the work, listening to it, or in explaining its meaning and beauty to others. To do this he will need much background information about the musical style of the time when it was composed and about Beethoven's relationship to those styles.

Another famous phrase is presented in Figure 3. Its basic harmony might be hypothetically distilled down to an implied A minor triad in the

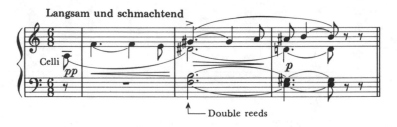

Figure 3: Wagner, *Tristan und Isolde*, Prelude

first measure, an augmented sixth with F in the bass in the second, and concluding in the third measure on a major-minor seventh chord with E as the root. Roman numerals can then be assigned within the apparent key of A minor; but again, as in the preceding example, such an analysis can be misleading, and in this case may simply be wrong. However, the analyst might proceed with this hypothesis, and would not be going astray if he concluded that the phrase ends on a half cadence in A minor. Going beyond the harmonic distillation, he might note that all the appoggiature have half step resolutions, that an important descending half step motive is found in the top voice and is reinforced by presentation in augmentation by the bassoon at its entrance on F in the second measure, that the phrase contains eight of the twelve tones of the chromatic scale, that the four which are missing (D flat-C, G-F sharp) also outline half step motives, and that the oboe presents the half step motive in inversion.

He would also do well to point out that the frequent half step appoggiatura, particularly the long one in the bass (second measure), is a significant germinal factor in the melodic, harmonic, and rhythmic structure of the work. Also, as the total work is studied, it will become apparent that the "French sixth" occurring momentarily on the last eighth note of the second measure is less important than the sound heard for the first five beats of the measure. The sonority heard throughout most of the measure is, indeed, a misspelled half-diminished seventh (E♯, G♯, B, D♯) in root position which, because of its significance in the overall shape of the *Prelude*, is sometimes called the "Tristan chord." It occurs at the climax of the *Prelude* (measure 83) and again in the concluding section. Thus the half-diminished seventh rather than the augmented sixth is the important structural agent apparent in this measure. (It now has become apparent that the initial harmonic description of an augmented sixth chord with F in the bass was essentially wrong.) Relating these things to the unfolding shape of the music, to certain aspects of the total opera, to Wagner's other works, and to the musical styles of the time will set the analyst on the road toward useful observations about the musical style of the *Prelude* to *Tristan und Isolde.*

Sometimes, out of a desire to be thorough, the analyst may find himself basing an analysis upon a false premise. This may come about through the mistaken application of some prescribed system, such as the use of twelve-tone analysis in a work which, it turns out, is not based upon that system. One can fall into such traps through well-meant attempts at inductive reasoning or *induction.* For example, the analyst may theorize that because a twentieth-century work is called "Sonata," it must in some way have been based upon the single movement form utilized so frequently in the eighteenth and nineteenth centuries. This may or may not be true, and if it is, the analyst is on the right track. If, however, he insists upon pursuing this line of reasoning in a work which has no relationship to the exposition, development, recapitulation pattern, his descriptive analysis will be meaningless. *Induction* is one of the basic tools of analysis, but the analyst must be sure that he has chosen the correct principle or concept and is not aborting the meaning or structure of a work in order to fit his analysis to a prescribed system.

Induction is essential in the analysis of twelve-tone music, at least at the level of pure description. But the analyst should be cautious, for it is surprisingly easy to find serial relationships which perhaps were not even subconsciously in the mind of the composer. This can result from the analyst's thinking in terms of pure pitches rather than line. Trying to fit a Bach fugue into a textbook pattern might also be a futile exercise, for many of them were not conceived in this fashion and should be neither performed nor heard as if they were. As we will learn in Chapters 3 and 4, real musical form is constantly fluctuating, changing, and growing within the rhythmic flow of the time-span of a composition; while preconceived formal matrices such as binary, rondo, and sonata form, though useful for labeling, are stereotypes which often do not correspond exactly to live pieces of music.

ANALYSIS OF CONTEMPORARY MUSIC

Analysis is more easily performed upon music of a fairly distant past than upon very recent music. Nevertheless, certain traditional concepts and methods are applicable to new music. Many contemporary composers have used traditional devices and the formal matrices of the past. It is very useful to determine what these concepts are and how they were utilized in order to define the uniquely innovative aspects of a composer's style.

For example, the first movement of Bartók's String Quartet No. Six can be validly analyzed as a sonata form. Through induction one can find virtually all of the essential features of the classical form in this work—translated to twentieth-century idioms, of course, through Bartók's unique style. The two themes shown in Figure 4 contain the basic motives of the first and second tonal groups of the sonata form, and their tonalities are appropriately contrasted by D and F, respectively.

Figure 4: Bartók, String Quartet No. 6, First Movement, Copyright 1941 by Hawkes and Son (London) Ltd; Renewed 1968. Reprinted by permission of Boosey & Hawkes, Inc.

But if the analyst contented himself with determining all of the features of the movement which show it to be a sonata form, he would be missing the point of analysis. Knowing that it is a sonata form may help superficially in the preparation of the work for performance—for example, in the interpretive treatment of certain important points of arrival such as the recapitulation or the coda. But what about the motivic structure of the movement, the contrapuntal, harmonic, and rhythmic styles, the tonal relationships, the textures, the unique string timbres, the frequently used intervals, the melodic style, the relationship of the movement and its introduction to the total work, its relation to Hungarian folk music, its place in Bartók's total output, and its relationship to other mid-twentieth-century styles? Finally and most importantly, how do these things contribute to the fact that this is a uniquely beautiful piece of music? These are the paramount concerns of the style analyst—musical phenomena far more meaningful than the discovery of relationships to structural stereotypes of the past.

Certain types of contemporary music seem to elude analysis. For example, in works by composers of chance music (Xenakis, Cage, and others) there is some question of the possibility of logical analysis, since there is some doubt as to the logical organization of such works. At the other extreme, music which is totally predetermined by some sort of schema is also difficult to analyze. In one sense it is almost pointless to describe the organization of a piece of music which has been totally controlled before its composition by serial techniques.* Since the composer has utilized a strict system applied to all elements of the music, analysis at the descriptive stage consists simply of elucidating that system. This should of course be done, but the ultimate evaluation should go beyond that description.

Another type of contemporary music that is difficult to analyze is the kind that can never again be recaptured in its original form—improvised music or music in which the performers' choices play a prime role. One of the most famous works of this type is *Piano Piece XI* by Karlheinz Stockhausen. In this work, even though the various sections of the piece are carefully notated, the composer requires that the performer choose the sequence of the sections, so that there are many possible outcomes. Theoretically, all of these possibilities could be subjected to analysis, but this may well be totally impractical.

Music which is composed entirely by electronic means and recorded on tape is usually difficult to analyze with any precision, simply because it seldom is written down in notation. There have been several attempts to devise satisfactory notational systems for electronic music, but these have rarely accomplished more than abbreviation or approximation of electronic sounds. Notation is most useful in works which combine conventional instruments or voices with electronic sounds, for the human performers are aided by graphic illustrations of electronic sounds in order to synchronize their entrances. The latter type of work is easier to analyze than pure electronic music and will be discussed later.

All of the types of contemporary music just discussed can and should be analyzed by some means reaching beyond mere description. After a thorough description has been accomplished, perhaps the best thing for the analyst to do is to listen to the work very carefully. In the case of chance and improvisatory works, the aural experience may be different each time it is performed (unless a performance has been recorded, in which case much of the justification for this kind of music is lost anyway). In any case, through careful listening, the analyst can plot such things as rough density profiles, peaks of tension and repose, and texture and timbre profiles. The same can be done for totally serialized works as well as pure electronic music. The point is that the real musical effect can be assessed through listening. Then, along with whatever descriptive data have been collected earlier, sufficient material should be available for a meaningful evaluation.

Among the analytical methods propounded in the twentieth century, that of Heinrich Schenker has exerted the strongest influence. His system

---

*The discussion of Babbit's *Composition No. 1 for Piano* in Chapter Six is a case in point.

begins with the assumption that, within the total musical texture, the composer has presented what can be called a foreground of his musical thought processes. The analyst's function, then, is to find the basic plan (primarily in harmonic and tonal terms) that lies behind that foreground—to find the underlying theme, as if the composition were a variation upon that unstated theme. Schenker analysis attempts to divine the *middleground* through the application of reductive techniques to the foreground, and finally the *background* through reduction of the *middleground*. It is a valid method, though a bit complex for general use. Also, since it is a system for analyzing tonal structure from a linear point of view, it is really applicable (according to Schenker, himself) only to music of the common practice period. (Some theorists are currently trying to find ways to apply it to twentieth-century music.) One of its drawbacks, from the point of view of the practicing musician, is that it tends to minimize fine details of the foreground, with the result that certain small but salient features essential to the beauty of a composition may be de-emphasized or ignored through the reductive process. The beginning analyst should be aware of this method for later study.

The analysis of form or shape is an important aspect of any analytical method. As the sounds of a piece of music unfold in time, a shape is gradually etched in our memories, much as a deep-powder skier leaves on the mountainside the visible evidence of his downhill trek. But in both instances the vestigial shapes, though interesting, do not possess the beauty of the moving events themselves. The flow of the music and the downhill ski run both occur in a time continuum, and their beauty is derived from the individual events themselves as well as from the composite of those events. But just as the skier's trail etched on the virgin snow is not the composite of his downhill run, so the remembered (or analyzed) shape of a piece of music is no more than a skeleton of its real composite beauty. The true beauty of music is found in the listener's experience of the individual events as they occur during the process of growth. It is these events which we remember. They articulate the musical flow, lend meaning to time, and thus define the shape or form of a musical work.

THE BASIC STEPS OF ANALYSIS

The skillful and creative analyst may devise a new analytical method for each piece of music he studies. Many aspects of music can be described by graphs and diagrams such as patterns of pitch profile, density, timbre, and texture; and graphs of tonal and rhythmic structure. If *all* of these are used, however, a finished analysis may turn out to be a confusing series of charts and diagrams. The analyst must select only those techniques which are valid, pertinent, and relevant to the work under study.

The process of analysis can be divided into two basic operations: Step I. Descriptive Analysis, and Step II. Synthesis and Conclusions.

Before undertaking descriptive analysis, however, the analyst should examine the general musical environment of the time when the work was composed. This preliminary step establishes a frame of reference—when the work was composed in relation to the composer's total output, where it falls in relation to geographical and historical influences, its text if it has one, events surrounding its composition, and other relevant background observations. Without the preliminary background stage, the normative practices of individual composers or historical periods or schools would be ignored. Meaningful judgments and comparisons to be made in the second step will rely on the background supplied at the outset.

The first step will be discussed in detail in the next chapter. The bulk of the real digging and descriptive analysis takes place at this stage. Small facts and details, of course, form the basis for conclusions. But it is possible to go into too much detail at this stage—to lose the forest for the trees. Here is where the perceptive and creative analyst is most selective in determining those observations which are most useful to the purposes of style analysis.

In the final stage, synthesis and conclusions, the analyst steps back and takes a long look, reviewing all observations up to that point and drawing together a meaningful evaluation of the total experience of the piece of music. The growth process, which will be discussed later, is of prime importance at this stage. Other broad considerations include the balance of unity and variety, judgments of the composer's imagination and resourcefulness, and external considerations such as the innovative qualities of the work, its overall evocative and emotional qualities, and its significance in music literature and history.

SUGGESTED ASSIGNMENTS

1. List several ways in which you, as a performer, composer, or scholar, have made useful stylistic judgments.

2. Find several stylistic norms based on music with which you are familiar from a brief period in music history or from the works of a single composer.

3. Cite several possible instances of inductive reasoning or induction, as well as possible misapplications of a prescribed system.

4. List several twentieth-century compositions which are clearly based upon styles or techniques of earlier periods. Describe the features of these works which reveal this.

5. Read published analyses, as assigned by instructor, of several well-known works of the standard repertoire.

2

The Analytical Method

In analyzing music it is best to begin with a clear-cut system or plan. This plan must be modified according to the nature of the work being analyzed, but it should have some features generally applicable to nearly all kinds of music. This chapter will be devoted to outlining such a system.

Any piece of music can be examined first in very fine detail, then in somewhat larger dimensions, and finally in terms of the total work. For descriptive analysis at these levels, let us use the terms (1) *microanalysis*, (2) *middle-analysis*, and (3) *macroanalysis*. Analysis at these three levels comprises the step of descriptive analysis mentioned in Chapter 1—the first basic analytical operation.

In actual practice a cursory macroanalysis should be performed before undertaking the three analytical levels in order. This helps place the more detailed observations in the proper frame of reference. Microanalysis includes detailed melodic, harmonic, and rhythmic analysis; form and texture at the smallest level; and small details of orchestration and timbre. The descriptions of the Beethoven and Wagner examples in the preceding chapter are examples of microanalysis. Middle-analysis deals with relationships between phrases and other medium-sized units and virtually anything that falls into neither the very large nor the very small categories. Macroanalysis begins with descriptions of things such as the instrumental or vocal medium and the total time duration, and proceeds to the less obvious such as the disposition of large events within this time span and broad harmonic, textural, and rhythmic considerations.

Obviously these dimensions of analysis may often overlap. Detailed harmonic analysis will ultimately lead to the uncovering of primary and secondary tonal centers, which will in turn lead to the discovery of tonal relationships in broader dimensions. In considering the role of an important motive in a cyclical work, its use in the total work must be considered.

13

Although we will categorize many of our observations in one of these three levels, their interrelationships must be remembered.

THE MUSICAL ELEMENTS

The next step in devising a system for analysis is to define the musical elements to be considered at the three analytical levels. They are (1) rhythm, (2) melody, (3) harmony, and (4) sound.* All musical events in a piece of music are combinations of these elements. *Rhythm*, the first element, includes not only matters of durations, accents, tempos, and meters, but also finite formal units such as phrases and periods. The second element, *melody*, includes every aspect of both rhythmic and pitch relationships in any single line. *Harmony*, the third element, includes not only chordal analysis and harmonic relationships, but also counterpoint or polyphony. The fourth element, called *sound* for want of a better term, includes timbre (and thus orchestration), dynamics, and texture. Again, as in the case of the three analytical levels, these four elements inevitably overlap.

GROWTH

Finally, we come to *growth*,† the moving shape of the music—the most important as well as the most elusive aspect of style analysis. The skiing analogy in Chapter One was intended to depict this generative process. It has to do with the manner in which the composer extends a musical composition—how he makes it flow through time. The movement of music through time is indeed like a flowing stream or river. Much of the meaning that a piece of music gives to a module of time is found in the gestures or events that occur at calculated points during its flow. Phrases defined by cadences, tonal relationships, affective qualities (psychological effects) of the musical elements, repose versus tension—all of these, occurring throughout the process of growth, define the shape or form of a piece of music.

Growth can be observed at any of the three analytical levels but is least apparent at the level of microanalysis. By trying to visualize himself as the composer in the midst of the compositional process, the analyst can see that at any point in this process the choices of how next to deploy the musical

---

*John White, *Understanding and Enjoying Music* (N.Y.: Dodd, Mead, 1968).
†Jan LaRue has used this term in a similar sense in *Guidelines for Style Analysis* (New York: W.W. Norton & Co., 1970).

elements are very wide indeed. For the analyst, this vast number of options can be distilled to four: (1) repetition, (2) development, (3) variation, (4) use of new material. So often will these terms be used, that for charting and annotating we will abbreviate them with R, D, V, or N. The element of contrast may be found in any of these, for even a repetition may be cast in a changed instrumentation, tonality, or tempo. But the nature of the contrast is of great interest to the style analyst, for herein is found the balance between a state of repose or composure (C) and forward motion, animation, or tension (T). The balance between repose and tension will be called CT;* at certain points one or more elements will be contributing to C while the others augment T. The element of harmony, for example, may occasionally be heightening the tension by a high level of dissonance at the same time that rhythm, melody, or sound are in a state of relative repose. Thus, CT must be analyzed in several sometimes conflicting layers. A profile of the CT factor may be diagrammed if it seems pertinent. This can be done in various ways by developing a scale of relative degrees of consonance and dissonance. An obvious method is to use a scale of 1 to 10 with 1 indicating the point of greatest repose and 10 the point of greatest tension. The level of the CT factor at any given point may be indicated simply by a number between 1 and 10.

The degree of organic unity (0) any material has within the total work is also determined by the nature of the contrasting material. In a general sense this term denotes a state of unity in which all of the parts contribute to the whole and in which none of the parts can exist independently. For musical purposes, however, organic unity can be defined as *the binding relationship among all the parts of a composition.* In a repetition with a changed instrumentation, this unity is clearly apparent in that all of the pitches, rhythms, and textures are the same. When completely new material is introduced, unity may be found in the relationship of the new material to another tempo, rhythm, melodic style, or instrumentation. Presumably, in a well-wrought piece of music, organic unity can be observed in any of its parts.

MICROANALYSIS

The analytical procedure requires that many annotations be made upon the actual pages of the score of the work being analyzed. The letter abbreviations presented in the foregoing will save time and space in

---

*Although RT might be more appropriate for this factor (Repose/Tension), C is used to represent *repose* in order to avoid confusion with R which will be used to represent *repetition.*

MACROANALYSIS

The macroanalysis chart which follows will serve as a guide for observation and description at the broadest level. Here the analyst draws upon all previous observation and description to describe the shape and growth of the work as a whole.

MACROANALYSIS CHART

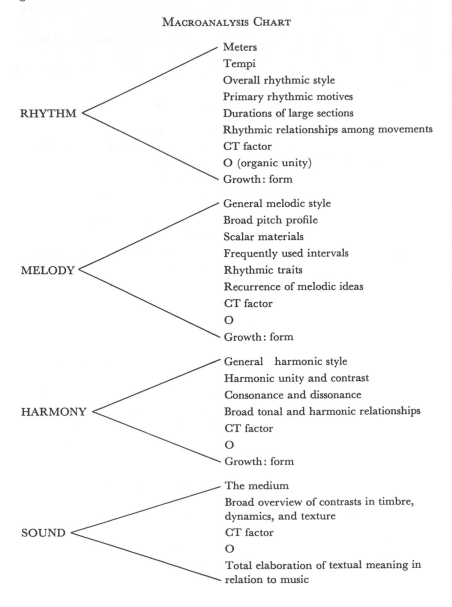

RHYTHM
- Meters
- Tempi
- Overall rhythmic style
- Primary rhythmic motives
- Durations of large sections
- Rhythmic relationships among movements
- CT factor
- O (organic unity)
- Growth: form

MELODY
- General melodic style
- Broad pitch profile
- Scalar materials
- Frequently used intervals
- Rhythmic traits
- Recurrence of melodic ideas
- CT factor
- O
- Growth: form

HARMONY
- General harmonic style
- Harmonic unity and contrast
- Consonance and dissonance
- Broad tonal and harmonic relationships
- CT factor
- O
- Growth: form

SOUND
- The medium
- Broad overview of contrasts in timbre, dynamics, and texture
- CT factor
- O
- Total elaboration of textual meaning in relation to music

The process of descriptive analysis outlined here will become operational and meaningful only when applied to real pieces of music. The next two chapters will furnish concepts and terminologies for the formal matrices which have been apparent in music of the past. Chapters 5 through 9 will elaborate upon the analysis of the four elements as applied to specific pieces of music from the Middle Ages to the twentieth century.

A DEMONSTRATION ANALYSIS

In order to make the analytical process more meaningful and applicable, there follows a finished sample analysis of a short keyboard work by Jean Phillippe Rameau. Although some of the terms used in this analysis will not be fully defined until later, it is important to see the analytical process in action from the start. Although the complete process of analysis will be used here, the final stage—synthesis and conclusions—will be discussed in greater detail in Chapter 10.

For the purpose of demonstration, this analysis is more complete than would normally be necessary. For the experienced musician, many of the observations of stylistic detail in this brief piece are so self-evident as to be superfluous. They are included here in order to furnish the beginning form and style analyst with a complete model to use as a point of departure for detailed analysis of more complex pieces of music. The complete score of the work being analyzed is shown in Figure 5.

ANALYSIS OF MINUET II IN G MINOR BY JEAN PHILLIPPE RAMEAU

Preliminary Background Material
The short Minuet II in G Minor was first published in 1731 in a collection of keyboard pieces by Jean Phillippe Rameau (1683-1764). It is paired with another short minuet preceding it in the key of G major. In typical baroque practice the first minuet would be performed again after the second one (without repeats) to create a da capo form. Rameau is a composer of the late baroque period and is often viewed as one of the culminating figures among baroque composers. Indeed, it was he who first codified the system of functional harmony in his *Treatise on Harmony* of 1722. At that time the idea of a key or tonal center defined by the relationship of the tonic and dominant triads was a well-established concept, but it had never been fully articulated in theoretical writings until Rameau's treatise. The system of formal architecture in which the shape of a piece of music is governed in large part by the relationship of the various cadence points to the home tonality became well established by the eighteenth century, and was the most important influence upon musical harmony and form for a period of at least two hundred years. Harmonically, then,

Rameau's music presents many of the normative practices of the late baroque. These norms include the concept that melody is rooted in harmony, the concept of modulation from and return to a home tonality or key, the concept of chordal inversion (the idea that a chord retains much of its characteristic function and identity regardless of which of its tones is in the bass), the concept of root movement of triads, and the system of primary triads. All of these were discussed in Rameau's treatise.

Rameau was French and was strongly influenced by Lully, the great French opera composer of the mid-baroque. Thus, there are many French traits in his music including the use of ornaments, the treatment of the French language in his operas, his use of the French overture form, and his predilection for dance movements. His operas are outwardly similar to Lully's but differ in harmonic and melodic style in that they are representative of the late baroque harmonic practices described in his treatise.

This short keyboard piece, undoubtedly intended for the harpsichord, is in binary form, the most important single movement chamber music form of the baroque. Rameau composed very little music until around 1723 and did not produce his first opera until ten years later. Although he had been a professional church organist for many years, he did not undertake composition as a career until he was about forty. Thus, this minuet must be classed as an early work in Rameau's total output.

I. Descriptive Analysis

A cursory macroanalysis reveals the work to be a single movement binary form in G minor. The phrase structure is very symmetrical and is clearly defined by the cadences. At first glance it does not appear to be a *rounded* binary form. Keyboard ornaments are frequent. There are no dynamic markings. The harmonic structure appears to be conventional with little or no modulation.

(A) Microanalysis (See annotations on score in italics)

Rhythm: Tempo not indicated, but should be andante or allegretto. Triple meter, motivic construction with two motives.

Slow harmonic rhythm: tonic held for three bars (1–3 and 9–11), dominant held for four bars (17–20). Fast harmonic rhythm only at final cadence (bar 31).

Little or no cross rhythm. No note values smaller than eighth note except for sixteenth notes in bar 20.

Rhythmically active but steady and unvaried. Eighth-note and quarter-note motion predominate.

Melody: Melodic intervals are predominately diatonic and conjunct (stepwise). Motive 1 conjunct, motive 2 disjunct (containing leaps), scale passage at bar 5 and later. Conjunct motion predominates, the major exceptions being the appearances of motive 2 and the broken style in bars 30–31.

Top voice (soprano) restricted to vocal range.

Melodic interest also in bottom voice but not in inner voices.

Conventional cadence structure.

Harmony: Dominant and tonic triads predominate in a slow harmonic rhythm. Not a dissonant movement. Frequent melodic passing tones, a few seventh chords mostly on V, a few suspensions (bars 4 & 12).
One diminished seventh (bar 20).
Contrary motion between outer voices in motive 2.
Free melodic inversion of motive 1 at bars 25–27.
Frequent contrary motion between outer parts.
Sound: Predominately close texture in typical baroque keyboard style.
Dynamics at discretion of performer, but if played on harpsichord would call for relatively little dynamic contrast.
No real bass until bar 9.
Only the top line remains intact as a voice throughout (melody).
Texture varies from a single line (bar 17) to as many as five simultaneous tones (bar 30).
Unison in bars 25–28.
Contrast in timbre would be at the discretion of the harpsichordist but, in any case, should be slight.

(B) Middle-analysis (See annotations on score in Roman face.)

Rhythm: Symmetrical four-bar phrase structure throughout.
Rhythmic growth achieved primarily by R.
Little rhythmic tension.
Melody: Melodic shape and growth achieved by R and D of motives at different pitch levels.
Phrases closely linked by half cadences.
CT remains rather even throughout except for bar 20 (high tension) and bar 28 (point of repose).
Harmony: Because of the relatively small harmonic vocabulary (almost entirely primary triads) and because all of the cadences except the final one are half cadences, the overall psychological effect is one of relative repose (C) or low tension. Harmonically, T is highest at bar 20 because of the diminished seventh, lowest at bar 28.
Sound: Considerable contrast and CT achieved by variety of texture.

(C) Macroanalysis (See annotations on score in boldface.)

Rhythm: The movement is in binary form, the first section consisting of an eight-bar period and its written-out repetition with varied texture (could be called a variant), the second being a sixteen-bar double period with a repeat sign.
O achieved by repetition of rhythmic ideas (motives).
Rhythmically symmetrical throughout.
Very little rhythmic development.
High point of T at bar 20 achieved primarily by increased rhythmic activity.
Low point at 28 achieved by lack of activity.
Melody: Diatonic throughout with stepwise motion predominating.
Motive 1 is the most striking melodic idea.
Ornaments add interest.
High B-flat occurs three times. Its use in bar 25 is effective because its most recent previous use was at bar 11.
Melodic element contributes little to CT.
O achieved by repetition and development of melodic ideas.

Harmony: Highly unified because of economy of harmonic materials, but also rather uninteresting harmonically for the same reason.

Not a rounded binary form but a strong feeling of harmonic return is created at bar 25.

Harmonic usage and phrase and cadence structure typical of late baroque binary form.

Non-modulating.

Contrapuntal devices such as melodic inversion of motive 1 create greater interest and add to 0.

Overall tonal structure conventional, although the absence of an authentic cadence until the end is a bit unusual (less so in pieces of shorter duration like this one).

Sound: Greatest textural contrast is achieved by unison passage in bars 25–28.

Element of sound not important.

II. Synthesis and Conclusions

This short dance movement is a highly unified example of a typical binary form* of the mature baroque. Unity, of course, is not a great problem in such a brief movement. It is short enough that modulation is not necessary for tonal contrast, which lends to the movement the additional unity of never departing from the key of G minor. Its standard form, its brevity, and the fact that it is a stylized dance form of the baroque all add to the organic unity; but within this framework the most important unifying feature is the use of motive 1 in various forms throughout the movement. The use of this motive at the beginning of the second section (bars 17-20) is particularly attractive and leads very convincingly to the high point of the movement at measure 20.

Free inversions of motive 1 are used at measure 25. The strong half cadence in measure 24, the change in texture to a unison at measure 25, and the use of the highest pitch in the total melodic range of the movement at bar 25 cause these final statements of motive 1 to possess a strong feeling of *return*, as in a rounded binary form. Because this return does not really present the opening material except in a highly varied form, the movement cannot properly be called a rounded binary form. In spite of this, the return at bar 25 is most convincing, lending to the total movement a feeling of motion toward this point. This satisfying arrival is then convincingly capped in the final four bars through use of the B material. The increased speed of the harmonic rhythm in the next to the last bar, and the trill which increases the density, makes it easy for the performer to use a slight ritard in the final cadence.

One of the beautiful features of this little movement is the fact that, by virtue of Rameau's techniques of varying and developing, the various

---

*Another logical viewpoint is to call this a bar form in which the first 16 measures is A-A *(Stollen-Stollen)*, while the 16 measures after the repeat sign is the extended B or *Abgesang*. Nevertheless, the material of the *Abgesang* is clearly derived from A which perhaps justifies the rationale for the monothematic binary form.

Figure 5: Rameau, Minuet II in G Minor

presentations of motive 1 never become dull. For example, the motive's ascent in bars 17-19 is answered by its descent (free inversion) in bars 25-27—simple, logical, and attractive. There is, of course, other thematic material in the movement; but the other ideas, such as motive 2 and the scalewise material of B (bar 5), function primarily to set off the presentations of motive 1 and do not serve as germinal elements.

Rhythmic and harmonic growth is not an important feature of the movement, although both rhythm and harmony contribute more than melody to the point of highest tension at bar 20. The elements of rhythm and harmony do, of course, shape the movement into a binary form consisting of two 16-bar sections: A B   A B   ‖: A(D)   B(D)   A(D)   B(D)   :‖

(The Ds in parentheses indicate development of A and B. If preferred, A'B'A'B' could be used for simplification.)

In summary, the movement is a distinguished example of a baroque binary form. French elements are found in the use of the dance form and in the ornamentations (*agréments*). Its rhythmic and harmonic growth process and its shape are not unique, either for Rameau or for the time in which it was written. Nevertheless, because of the composer's imaginative use of motive 1, the simple stylized form emerges as a movement of real delight.

*   *   *   *   *   *

As previously stated, this analysis was deliberately written in an overly detailed manner in order to furnish a model for the analysis of more complex pieces later. Even so, numerous small details have been passed over, simply because they add nothing significant to our understanding of the music. For example, none of the many diatonic passing tones in the melody were identified in the microanalysis because none of them are in any way unique. The words "frequent melodic passing tones" under the harmony heading in the microanalysis sufficiently describe them. Likewise, none of the raised sixth and seventh scale degrees are mentioned under the harmony headings because it is self-evident that they are being used in the conventional diatonic manner. The one minor dominant triad in bar 23 is not mentioned in step II because it is used in a perfectly normal manner in first inversion with a descending bass line. (It is identified by annotation in the score.) In this case, even the cadence qualities do not add much to our understanding of the movement as a unique piece of music (though they are annotated on the score and mentioned in the macroanalysis). It is important to remember that description of small insignificant details can easily detract from the important features that should be emphasized. In the Rameau Minuet the most important feature is motive 1—how the composer treats it and how its treatment is essential to the unity and beauty of the movement. To have overemphasized other less significant details would have diverted attention from the most meaningful features of the analysis. Note also that in step II it is appropriate to make subjective value judgments—to comment on the beauty and unity of a work. Likewise, if the analyst finds flaws in a work— if its repetitions are deadly or if it lacks organic unity—step II is the place to say so.

SUGGESTED ASSIGNMENTS

1. Describe the harmonies (harmonic microanalysis) of a passage containing chromatic harmonies from a nineteenth-century composition.
2. For the same passage, draft a CT profile according to the plan suggested in this chapter.
3. Describe the factors contributing to the organic unity (0) of a brief movement from an eighteenth-century composition.
4. Perform "cursory macroanalyses" on several brief instrumental movements of the classical period.
5. Attempt to perform a complete analysis of a simple eighteenth-century instrumental movement, using the analysis of the Rameau Minuet as a model.

3

Substructural Units of Music

Music comes alive in the hands of that composer whose musical ideas themselves furnish the shaping force of the music. The reader is advised to refer to Ernst Toch's book *The Shaping Forces in Music* (Criterion Music Corp., 1958) for an excellent description of the manner in which small thematic fragments called *motives* generate musical growth. As demonstrated in the analysis of the Rameau Minuet in the preceding chapter, the growth process thrives on the motive—upon its repetitions and transformations, and upon its power to control the shape of a complete work of art.

MOTIVES

The motive is the smallest structural unit possessing thematic identity. It is not necessarily complete in itself, for often a melodic phrase may be constructed of several motives. A motive's thematic identity may be found in the intrinsic qualities of its rhythm or its pitches, or in both combined. There is no hard and fast rule regarding the maximum number of tones permitted in the defining of a motive; but since a motive must consist of at least an *arsis* and a *thesis*, there are no motives with fewer than two tones. The term *arsis* refers to what we frequently call an upbeat or anacrusis in conventional rhythm, while *thesis* is the downbeat. Other writers have compared the *arsis-thesis* phenomenon to inhaling and exhaling, or lifting up the foot and putting it down. Figure 6 is an example containing a two-note motive consisting of a whole note moving down a half step to a quarter note. The melodic progression of a descending half step would not necessarily possess the thematic identity necessary to create a true motive, but in this famous example the motive's identity is reinforced several times by means of repetition and inversion, as shown by the brackets.

Motives of two tones are infrequently found, and motives of more than

26

Figure 6: Sibelius, *Finlandia*, Op. 26

six tones are also rather rare. The seven-tone motive from the Machaut Mass (Figure 7) is an example of the longer type. As with most motives, this one contributes much to the organic unity of the Mass by its use throughout all the movements of the work.

Figure 7: Motive of the Machaut Mass

A motive's importance to a total musical structure can be determined only by surveying and appraising its use throughout the work. Indeed, unless a thematic fragment is used significantly in the course of a piece of music it should not be called a motive, for the word itself conveys the idea of a shaping force or structural element. It was inevitable that throughout Western history (and undoubtedly in the music of other cultures, as well) motives were used to hold pieces of music together—to give them organic unity. Probably the short melodic patterns of ancient Greek music (*nomoi*) functioned as motives in the heterophonic music of that culture, serving a purpose similar to that of the motive in Figure 7 in the Machaut Mass.

Often enough, a motive's identity may be hidden or underplayed in its earliest presentations at the beginning of a work, only to be revealed in its full structural or developmental power later on in the composition. This is well illustrated in the opening theme of the Allegro first movement (following the slow introduction) of Haydn's Symphony No. 104, the "London" Symphony (Figure 8). Here the six-note motive marked by a bracket in the

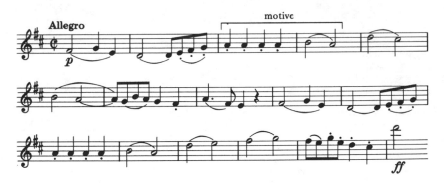

Figure 8: Haydn, Symphony No. 104, Opening Theme of the Allegro First Movement

example sounds quite unobtrusive and insignificant as a part of the opening melody. In fact, in the entire exposition section it is used only as a part of the melody and not as an important structural element. It is only in the development section (after the repeat sign) that this six-note motive reveals itself as the most important thematic germ of the movement. Then Haydn demonstrates his prodigious structural and developmental skill by using nothing but this motive throughout the development section.

Brahms used a technique similar to that of Haydn in his Symphony No. 2, but he used it in all four movements and with a greater effort at transformation of the motive throughout the work. Some analysts, in fact, have argued that nearly all of the thematic material in the entire symphony can be traced to the three-note motive presented quietly and unobtrusively by the basses and cellos in the opening measure of the first movement (Figure 9). A few of the more notable instances of the thematic transformation of this motive are shown in Figure 10.

Figure 9: Brahms, Symphony No. 2, Opening of First Movement

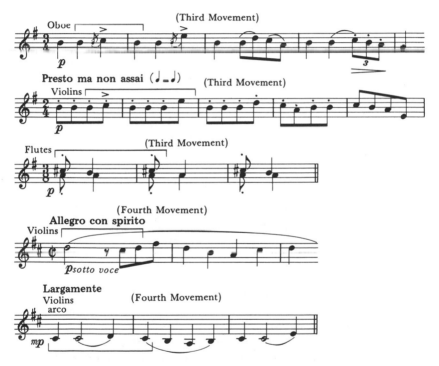

Figure 10: Brahms, Symphony No. 2, Excerpts

We have seen Rameau's use of the motive in the short binary form analyzed in the preceding chapter. His contemporaries in the baroque period used motives in similar ways, often with much repetition and little genuine development. J. S. Bach, for example, used a motive like the one in Figure 11 in many of his instrumental compositions, repeating it many times in succession at different pitch levels within a triadic context to build melodic, harmonic, or polyphonic fabrics. Bach's "bricklaying" with this motive can be seen in the first movements of the third and sixth Brandenburg Concertos, in the first movement of the third viol da gamba sonata, and in several other works. This particular motive was obviously one of his favorites, but the same technique applied to other short motives can be seen in many of his other instrumental works.

Figure 11

The five-tone motive in Figure 12 from the first movement of the Ravel String Quartet is an example of a motive which derives its identity from both the rhythmic and the pitch elements. In the course of the movement the rhythm of the quarter note followed by two eighth notes is used frequently, and the ear clearly relates it to this opening measure even though the original pitch pattern is not followed. The descending whole step is also an important melodic element in its recurrences throughout the movement.

Figure 12: Ravel, String Quartet, First Movement. Instrumental Parts published by Société Musicale G. Astruc & Cie. c. 1903.

Although some melodies are very obviously constructed out of one or two motives which recur frequently, this does not mean that all melodies are built of motives. Some melodies are constructed in a through-composed manner with little or no repetition of small thematic fragments. Even when a rhythmic or melodic fragment is repeated it should not be called a motive unless the analyst's ear tells him that the nature, quantity, and quality of the repetitions indicate that the fragment is of real structural importance in the music. Sometimes such a judgment is not easy to make. In examining the Caccini example in Figure 13, the sharp-eyed analyst would probably notice the similarity between the first three notes in the voice part and the second, third, and fourth notes in the bass line. Then, if the analyst were really determined, he might also find an overlapping statement of the fragment at the end of the first bar of the voice part, an inversion in the second measure

Figure 13: Caccini Madrigal

of the voice part, and even a retrograde inversion of the fragment in the last three notes of the bass line! Although there may be room here for valid differences of opinion, most theorists would probably agree that this is carrying motivic analysis just a bit far. There are a number of factors which should lead the analyst to the conclusion that this three-note fragment should not be called a motive and that the recurrences of the three-note fragment, though perhaps not really accidental, do not constitute significant structural use of a melodic pattern. These judgmental factors could include aspects of Caccini's personal style as well as the normative practices of the period around 1600, when this piece was written. But the most important factor is the sound of the music, and the analyst's ear should lead him to the conclusion that there is no clearly identifiable motive in this example and that the composer was not consciously utilizing the technique of motivic structure.

A motive very similar to the three-note fragment in the Caccini example is found at the beginning of the exposition of the first movement of Bartók's String Quartet No. Six (see Figure 14). In the Bartók example, however, it is perfectly clear that the composer is consciously using various forms of a three-note motive consisting of a minor second and a perfect fourth (or fifth in intervallic inversion). This is clear even from the short excerpt and is borne out even further in the course of the movement. The analyst's knowledge of Bartók's style would lead him to look for motivic structure in this composer's music, whereas in Caccini's time, this sort of technique would have been most unusual.

On another tack, however, there are melodic fragments which do recur in the course of a piece of music in such a way as to leave no doubt of the composer's intentions, but which still should not be called motives because they are not really significant in the structure of the work. Such fragments can be called *figures*. *Figures* or *figurations* may often occur in accompaniment passages or in transitional or connective material designed to link two sections together. Examples of accompaniment figures are most numerous and can be found in virtually any keyboard or ensemble work of the classical period as well as in the music of other periods. One such example is shown in Figure 15. Figurations formed of connective material are much less common; quite often what appears to be such a figuration may in fact be derived

Figure 14: Bartók, String Quartet No. 6, First Movement, Copyright 1941 by Hawkes and Son (London) Ltd; Renewed 1968. Reprinted by permission of Boosey & Hawkes, Inc.

Figure 15: Schubert, Octet, Op. 166

Figure 16: Mozart, Symphony in G Minor

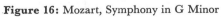

from an important motive stated earlier and thus should be classed as motivic material rather than a figuration. However, occasionally a composer may use connective material which, at least outwardly, does not appear to be related to motivic material. Such a figuration is found in the sixth bar of the excerpt in Figure 16. This figuration happens to recur at the parallel point in the recapitualation of the movement but still does not have the structural significance necessary for it to be called a motive.

PHRASES AND CADENCES

Although the motive is the smallest structural unit in music, the *phrase* is the smallest musical unit which conveys a more or less complete musical thought. Phrases vary in length and are terminated at a point of full or partial repose, which is called a *cadence*. The melodic and harmonic nature of the cadence determines the level or degree of repose at the cadence point. A more or less standard terminology has grown up around the cadence types in common use during the seventeenth, eighteenth, and nineteenth centuries. This terminology will be most useful in describing and labeling the cadences of the music of that period.

Figure 17

Beethoven, Piano Sonata, Op. 13

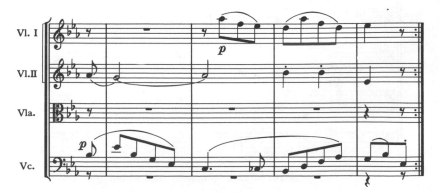

Beethoven, Symphony No. 3

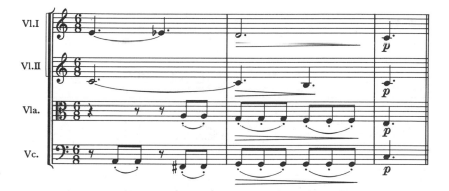

Haydn, String Quartet, Op. 54, No. 1

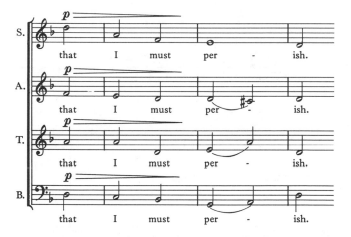

Brahms, German Requiem, No. III

Figure 18

Tchaikovsky, Symphony V, Op. 64

Gluck, *Orphée*, Act II, Scene 1

Pachelbel, Fughetta for the Magnificat

The cadence type which evokes the strongest feeling of finality or conclusiveness at the end of a phrase is the *perfect authentic cadence*. The word *authentic* indicates that the harmonic progression is that of the dominant (or VII) to the tonic, while the word *perfect* indicates that the root of the triad is found in both the bass voice and the top voice of the tonic triad with which the phrase ends. Several perfect authentic cadences are shown in Figure 17.

An *imperfect* authentic cadence, then, is one in which the final tonic triad is in a position with a tone other than the root in the bass voice and/or the top voice of the texture. Obviously, there are several possible varieties of imperfect authentic cadences. The most common type is one in which the final tonic triad is in fundamental or root position with either the third or fifth in the top voice. This is a somewhat less conclusive cadence than the perfect authentic. When an imperfect authentic cadence is created by casting the final tonic triad in an inversion (a rare variety), the lack of finality is even more marked. Figure 18 shows several examples of imperfect authentic cadences. Based as they are on the progression of V to I, all types of authentic cadences evoke greater feelings of repose or finality than do other cadence types.

A *half cadence* is any cadence which concludes on the dominant triad. Because of the V triad's quality of unrest—of expectation for a subsequent arrival on the tonic—the half cadence creates a very inconclusive feeling. Several half cadences are shown in Figure 19.

Figure 19

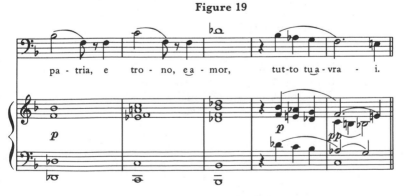

pa - tria, e   tro - no, e a - mor,   tut-to tu a - vra - i.

Verdi, *Aida*, Act III

37

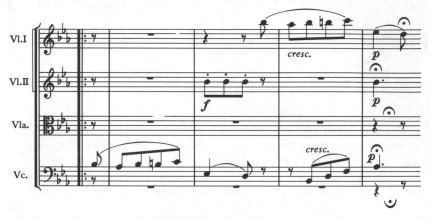

Beethoven, Symphony No. 3

Bach, Chorale: *Es Wollt uns Gott*

A half cadence may consist of virtually any combination of chords approaching the dominant. However, when the chord progression of a half cadence in the minor mode is IV⁶–V or II⁴₃–V, this type of half cadence is often called the *phrygian cadence*. Its derivation from the *clausula vera* of the

Figure 20: Bach, Chorale: *Schau Lieber Gott*

phrygian mode is illustrated by the motion of the outer parts in the example of Figure 20.

A cadence which has all the traits of an authentic cadence except that the final chord is not the tonic is called a *deceptive cadence*. Obviously, it is called *deceptive* because the dominant does not progress to a final tonic as it does in the authentic cadence, but instead goes to another chord, usually to VI. The unique psychological effect of this cadence leaves the listener with a feeling of surprise, inconclusiveness, and expectation. An example of the deceptive cadence is shown in Figure 21.

Figure 21: Bach, Chorale: *Christ Lag in Todesbanden*

The *plagal cadence* consists of the progression IV–I (rarely II⁶–I). It may be perfect or imperfect according to the same criteria as the authentic cadence. It also has some of the same feeling of finality as the authentic cadence, but because the progression IV–I does not have the strong tonal implications of V–I (without its leading tone), its ability to define a tonality is considerably less. Much less frequent than the authentic cadence, its most common usage is in the "Amen" cadence used at the ends of hymns in many churches. An unusual example of the plagal cadence is shown in Figure 22.

Figure 22: Tchaikovsky, *Romeo and Juliet*, Overture-Fantasy

When a cadence concludes on a strong beat of a measure (1 or 3 in duple or quadruple meter, 1 in triple meter) it is described as a *masculine cadence*. The term *feminine cadence* is used to describe a cadence which concludes on the weak beat of the measure. Although descriptions of gender may seem inappropriate, these terms have come into general use for describing cadences of Western music. The Verdi excerpt in Figure 19 would be described as a feminine cadence, while all of the others in examples 17 to 22 are masculine cadences.

PHRASE STRUCTURE

Each of these examples of cadence types has illustrated a clearcut phrase ending. Not all phrases are so clearly defined. Sometimes the new phrase may begin at the same point as the conclusion or cadence of the preceding phrase to create what is called a *phrase elision*. An example of phrase elision is shown in figure 23.

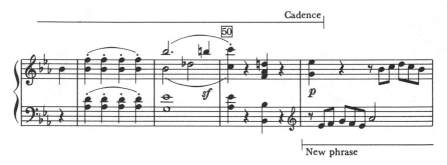

Figure 23: Beethoven, Piano Sonata, Op. 13

Another method of extending a melody, closely related to phrase elision, is to delay the cadence. That is, the phrase is constructed in such a way as to prepare the listener for the cadence at a certain point, but then unexpectedly the music continues to a cadence later on. At certain points in some kinds of music the texture may be so developmental in nature that there may be no phrase structure apparent at all. Other works, particularly some fugues, may have no clear-cut cadences because all the phrases overlap; or they may be composed in a completely continuous texture with an almost total absence of phrase structure throughout the entire composition.

In music not based upon the normative harmonic practices of the "common practice" period, devices other than these cadence types are used to define the end of a phrase or cadence. Often in twentieth-century music rhythm may be used in such a way as to create a feeling of repose comparable to that of a cadence. In other instances simply a pause in the continuity may achieve the same result. The elements of harmony or melody may also define cadences in twentieth century music, even though the devices used may be unrelated to the conventional cadence types of earlier music. It is important to remember that melody is a prime moving force in music through the ages; and vital to melody, regardless of style, is the contrast of forward motion to points of full or partial repose. Thus, the feeling of phrases and cadences is as important to contemporary music as to eighteenth- and nineteenth-century music. To illustrate one type of twentieth-century phrase structure, let us examine the opening of the second movement of Bartók's Second String Quartet (Figure 24).

Figure 24: Bartók, String Quartet No. 2, Opening of Second Movement. Copyright 1920 by Universal Edition A.G.; Renewed 1948. Copyright and renewal assigned to Boosey & Hawkes, Inc., for the U.S.A. Reprinted by permission.

Figure 25: Dallapiccola, *Quaderno Musicale di Annalibera*, Final Movement, Quartina. © Copyright 1953 by Edizioni Suvini Zerboni S.p.A., Corso Europa 5/7, Milano, Italy. Used By Permission of Boosey & Hawkes, Inc., Sole Agents.

The eighth rest in bar 3 and the quarter rest in bar 5 of the Bartók example may suggest the possibility of three phrases. But the rhythm and tempo, and particularly the sixteenth notes, give these rests a quality of urgency which pulls the three fragments together into a seven-bar phrase. All the elements play a role in defining the cadence at bar 7. The arrival at the perfect fifth in bar seven (the E-flat is an appoggiatura) after the emphasis on the diminished fifth creates a feeling of harmonic repose and also establishes a tonal center of D. The rhythmic tension of the sixteenth notes early in the phrase is alleviated by the steady drive of eighth notes to the final chord. Sound also plays its part, particularly in the crescendo created by the doublings and the fortissimo final chord; while the overall melodic contour lends to this phrase the character of a single emphatic gesture.

Figure 25 illustrates another twentieth-century way of delineating phrase structure in the final movement of Luigi Dallapiccola's *Quaderno Musicale di Annalibera* (later transcribed as *Variations for Orchestra*). Not unlike the accompanied monody of the early seventeenth century, this brief movement is a good example of accompaniment and melody in a twelve-tone work. The title *Quartina* refers to a four-line verse, like a quatrain, and each of the four lines can be viewed as a musical phrase. The two basic factors which contribute to this phrase structure are (1) the harmonic logic of the piece, for each line contains two simultaneously presented forms of the tone row, one in the melodic line and one in the accompaniment; and (2) the overall contour of each line of the melody, for the cadence feeling at the end of each line is unmistakable. Each line is a discrete harmonic and melodic unit which creates the effect of four separate musical gestures or phrases.

Although many phrases are in symmetrical lengths of two or four bars, particularly in music of the eighteenth century, there are nevertheless many examples of phrases of three, five, or seven bars, even in music of the classical period. Four-bar phrases can be very beautiful, but because of their predictability, it is also possible for them to become dull and uninteresting. Mozart more than Haydn was inclined toward the frequent use of four-bar phrases, but by his ingenious combinations of phrases into groups or periods and

Figure 26: Mozart, Piano Sonata in F, K. 332, First Movement

because of his phenomenal melodic gift, his melodies are seldom dull. Figure 26 presents the opening theme from Mozart's F Major Piano Sonata, K. 332. This theme can be described as a phrase-group consisting of three four-bar phrases, but note that each of the phrases is totally different from the others in regard to cadence type, rhythm, and melodic style. The quality of melodic freedom thus created offsets the symmetry of the four-bar phrases.*

A good proportion of the phrases in Haydn's music are made up of odd numbers of bars. The famous example in Figure 27 is from a *Feldpartita*, a military piece for wind band which Brahms used as the theme for his *Variations on a Theme of Haydn*, Op. 56. The example consists of two five-bar phrases in an *antecedent-consequent* relationship. That is, though the phrases are melodically similar, the half cadence at the end of the first phrase is answered by

Figure 27: Haydn, *Feldpartita*

the authentic cadence at the end of the second; and the melodic differences between the two are related to this cadence structure. One of the charms of this melody, and perhaps the very quality that attracted Brahms to it, is the use of five-bar phrases. If the third bar of each phrase is deleted to reduce them to conventional four-bar phrases, it is readily apparent that the four-bar version is less interesting, rhythmically and melodically, than the original.

PERIOD AND PHRASE-GROUP STRUCTURE

We have already seen an example of a period (Figure 27) and a phrase-group (Figure 26). A period is a structure of two consecutive phrases, often built of similar or parallel melodic material, in which the first phrase gives the impression of asking a question which is answered by the second phrase. Usually the interrogative or antecedent effect of the first phrase is created by the inconclusive nature of the cadence, which often is a half cadence; while the affirmative or consequent effect of the second phrase is usually created by concluding it with an authentic cadence. Figure 27 is a classic example of a period in which the first phrase concludes with a half

---

*Surely it is unnecessary to point out that, while the cadences delineate the four bar phrases, the phrases are also divisible into 2 plus 2.

cadence (bar 5) answered by an authentic cadence at the end of the second. Also, this is an example of the more common type of period in which the two phrases are built of parallel melodic material. The differences between the two phrases result from the two types of cadences.

Figure 28: Beethoven, Piano Sonata in C Minor, Op. 13 (*Pathétique*), Second Movement

The famous example in Figure 28 is also a period. Its four-bar phrase length is more conventional than that of the preceding example, but because the second phrase is built of new melodic material (rather than parallel material) it is less conventional and gives the effect of greater freedom of melodic thought. Perhaps this is why the Beethoven example is more evocative and, if you will, of greater lyrical beauty.

Although the dominant-tonic pattern of Figures 27 and 28 is by far the most common, periods may be found in a variety of tonal structures, and they may modulate away from the key in which they begin. Rhythmically, Figure 28 represents the norm during the eighteenth and nineteenth centuries, for the vast majority of periods are constructed of two four-bar phrases. Nevertheless, as we have seen in Figure 27, there are instances of periods of greater length. In a fast tempo a period may occur quite naturally in a pattern of sixteen bars. Also either phrase may be extended by various devices, and either phrase may be repeated literally. Phrase repetition most frequently occurs with the antecedent phrase, although there are instances of repetition of the consequent. When phrase repetition occurs, this means that there are more than two phrases in the period. But the essential trait of a period, even in an exceptional instance, is that it possess a clear two-part structure (usually in two parallel phrases) with a feeling of antecedent and consequent between the two parts, usually achieved by means of the harmonic element. A group of three or more phrases linked together without the two-part feeling of a period (as in Figure 26) can be termed a *phrase-group*. Phrase-group is also the appropriate label for a pair of consecutive phrases in which the second is the repetition of the first or in which, for whatever reason, the antecedent-consequent relationship is absent.

Figure 29: Beethoven, Symphony No. 7 in A, Op. 92, Second Movement

A *double period* is a group of at least four phrases (occasionally more than four) in which the first two phrases form the antecedent and the third and fourth phrases together form the consequent. The example in Figure 29 is a double period in which the second phrase modulates to the relative major and concludes with an authentic cadence in that key. The cadence on the mediant of the original key of A minor creates the inconclusive effect essential to an antecedent. The two consequent phrases then modulate back to A minor for a perfect authentic cadence in the original key.

Figure 30 is an example of a double period which concludes with a

Figure 30: Mendelssohn, *Songs Without Words*, Op. 85, No. 1

Figure 31: Schubert, Quintet in A Major (*Trout*), Fourth Movement

modulation. In this case the antecedent effect is achieved by means of a half cadence at the end of the second phrase. The consequent, in spite of its modulation, is a convincing response to the antecedent. In many double periods the first and third phrases are similar or identical, which adds to the organic unity of the structure.

Both of the preceding examples of double periods are in the normative pattern of sixteen bars. Figure 31 is an example of a formal structure which has the characteristics of a double period, but which is considerably longer, not only because of the repeat of the first eight bars, but also because of the written-out repetition of the fourth phrase to add a fifth phrase to the structure. Some writers have termed this type of enlarged double period an *incipient binary* form. The three factors essential to this form are (1) greater length, (2) a strong half cadence (i.e., with a secondary leading tone) or modulation to the key of the dominant (or other related key such as the relative major) at the end of the first section, and (3) that the structure stands alone as a complete musical entity. In this example the length factor is more than satisfied by the repeat sign and the additional phrase. There may be some room for disagreement regarding the modulation to the dominant at the end of the first section. It might be argued that since the G-sharp occurs only in the seventh bar and is not confirmed by later repetitions, this is a half cadence in the home tonality (V/V—V) rather than an authentic cadence in the key of the dominant. Perhaps so, but this is too subjective a distinction to be insistent about. In this case because of the length of both sections, because there is at least a strong half cadence, if not a modulation to A at the end of the first section, and because the structure stands alone as a complete musical entity, the label of incipient binary form is justified.

SUGGESTED ASSIGNMENTS

1. Find motives and trace their use throughout a given movement or extended work. Do this for representative works of the baroque, classical, and romantic periods, and for a twentieth-century composition.

2. Find several examples of all types of cadences in the music of the eighteenth and nineteenth centuries.

3. Find examples of phrase elision and delayed cadences in eighteenth- and nineteenth-century music.

4. Discuss the methods by which phrase structure and cadence feeling are achieved in a specific twentieth-century composition.

5. In the literature of the classical and early romantic periods, find and analyze the phrase structure of examples of period, double period, phrase-group, and incipient binary form.

4

Normative Structures

As the title indicates, this chapter will be devoted to those shapes and structural units of music which have become part of our musical and analytical terminology through their stylized use in the history of Western music. What follows, then, will be a kind of taxonomy and description of the structural and formal stereotypes of Western music. It should be remembered, however, that these terms represent the normative practices of composers throughout the past two or three hundred years and that many pieces of music, even though they are clearly in one or another of these given forms, will depart significantly from the norms. Indeed, it is the departures from the norms which breathe the life of uniqueness into music, for it is only the mediocre composer who uses a traditional pattern simply as a mold to hold his musical ideas. In a sense, then, determining the stereotyped form or label for a piece of music is the very least that the analyst can do.

Examples of deviations from these norms are more common than the norms themselves in the actual literature of music. The purpose here is not to describe these unique deviations but to furnish the student with a taxonomy of labels to use as descriptive terms in analysis. Some writers on form have attempted to catalog the many variant ways in which these formal patterns have been used in the literature of eighteenth- and nineteenth-century music. Many of these commonly used variants are described in Wallace Berry's *Form in Music* (Prentice-Hall, Inc., 1966), an excellent and useful reference for the student of musical form.

It should be remembered that, for the most part, these formal patterns are not really important except as generic terms to use for description. What is significant is the growth process of the music and how the composer has filled the time span in which this process takes place with musical events which are coherent, meaningful (at various emotional or intellectual levels), and beautiful to the listener.

BINARY FORM

Having seen an example of an incipient binary form in the preceding chapter (Figure 31), let us proceed to the full binary, a form which was of great importance in the baroque and classical periods and well into the nineteenth century. The general shape and tonal pattern of a full binary form is identical to that of the incipient binary form, the primary distinction between the two being one of proportion. Not counting the repeat of the first section, the example in Figure 31 is only twenty measures in length with only two phrases in the first section. Generally speaking, a full binary form is larger than this. It may be a bit arbitrary to set exact limitations as to the minimum number of bars necessary for a movement to be called a full binary form, but as a general rule of thumb to which there may be exceptions, each of the two sections should contain at least three phrases. The diagram in Figure 32 shows the pattern of a binary form of the type found in the music of the seventeeth, eighteenth, and nineteenth centuries.

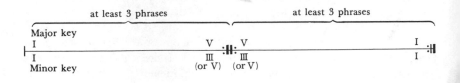

Figure 32

The Rameau minuet which served as the subject for the sample analysis at the end of Chapter 2 (Figure 5) is a typical example of the baroque binary form, and follows the above pattern in every detail. The repeat sign separating the two sections was used in the majority of binary forms of the seventeenth and eighteenth centuries. In performance these repeats are treated with great liberty. Indeed, at the discretion of the performer, one, both, or none of the repeats may be observed. Obviously, if both repeats are observed the form is considerably expanded, though its basic pattern remains the same.

The works of Rameau, Scarlatti, Couperin, Corelli, Vivaldi, Bach, Handel—indeed the works of virtually every instrumental composer of the middle and late baroque—are filled with binary forms of this sort. The pattern was normally used for the movements of the baroque dance suite (excepting preludes and galanteries) and the sonata da chiesa. Many baroque binary forms are based upon one or two thematic ideas or motives; and some of them (particularly those of Bach) are expanded to movements of considerable length. The form continued to be used in the classical and romantic periods, though it gradually began to be superseded in importance by the newer classical forms. The baroque binary differs from that of later periods in that continuous motivic structure or imitative texture was more common than clear phrase and period structure. The reverse was true in the classical period, when clearly delineated phrases with clear-cut cadences became a distinguishing feature of the style.

Examination of a number of binary forms will reveal that the second section is invariably longer than the first, and that often at the beginning of this section modulations to keys other than the dominant may occur. Obviously, within the matrix of the binary form there are a vast number of possible patterns of phrase, cadence, and tonal structures, and these differences are of prime importance in style analysis.

One important variant of the form is the pattern known as *rounded binary form*, in which there is a clear cut return to or restatement of the

Figure 33: Vivaldi, Sonata No. 1 for Cello and Continuo, First Movement

opening thematic material in its original key in the middle or shortly before the end of the second section. This return need not be complete but should be substantial enough and sufficiently like the opening to be identifiable as a restatement. To emphasize its formal significance it is usually prepared by some emphasis on the dominant in the moments just preceding the return to the tonic. It will be seen later that rounded binary form is an important step in the evolution of sonata form and that the return is comparable to the recapitulation of a sonata form. Certain baroque composers, including Bach and Handel, used the rounded binary form very infrequently. On the other hand, many rounded binary forms are found among the four-movement church sonatas of Vivaldi. One such example is shown in Figure 33.

THREE-PART FORMS

The concept of presenting a musical idea, departing from it to present contrasting material, and then returning to the original idea has been basic to musical form throughout Western history. In one way or another this concept can be seen in operation in sections of almost any piece of music, though not necessarily in the overall pattern of a movement. Obviously, it is an important feature of the rounded binary form just discussed; but it also can be seen in operation in incipient binary forms and even in brief double periods. In most if not all binary forms and double periods the contrasting material presented at the beginning of the second section (or period) is based in part upon the material of the first section, so that contrast is achieved by means of harmony, rhythm, motivic development, or texture, rather than by the presentation of entirely new melodic material.

Writers on musical form disagree as to what constitutes a true three-part form, particularly regarding the distinction between rounded binary form and *incipient ternary form*. It cannot be denied that there is some logical basis for labeling the example in Figure 33 as an incipient ternary form, viewing the section from the middle repeat sign to the return as the middle or "B" section. On the other hand, the binary division is clearly apparent and the degree of contrast, melodic or otherwise, is relatively slight in the section immediately following the repeat sign. It seems simpler and perhaps more logical to use the label *three-part form* or *ternary form* only when there is a middle section of substantial length built of substantially new thematic material. With this guideline we can use the term *rounded binary* in place of *incipient ternary form*, and reserve the term *three-part form* for movements in which there really is a full-fledged "B" section of new thematic material.

Happily for music, many pieces do not clearly fall into one category or another. The Handel Minuet in Figure 34, for example, might be called either a rounded binary or a three-part form depending upon the analyst's conclusions regarding the middle section from the repeat sign to the return.

Figure 34: Handel, Minuet in F Major

In any case, to the penetrating student of music, the label is far less important than the music itself, and the very fact that the form is not a clear stereotype is of real interest to the style analyst.

There are, however, many movements which can be unequivocally labeled as three-part forms. They are abundant among the short character pieces for piano of Schumann, Mendelssohn, Chopin, and other early romantic composers. The Schumann *Folk Song* in the Album for the Young

(Op. 68, No. 9) is a very clear example. The Chopin Prelude in D-Flat Major (Op. 28) is a more extended example in which the harmonic contrast of the middle section is achieved by change of mode to the parallel minor rather than by change of tonal center. Other examples can be found in the music of any period, even in the twentieth century, for the concept upon which three-part form is based is perhaps the simplest and most logical solution to achieving both unity and variety in short pieces of music.

The *da capo* device was often used to create extended three-part forms, as in the *da capo* aria of Neapolitan opera. Also, when two movements are linked together (as in dance pairs) both movements may be binary forms, but because of the *da capo* sign at the end of the second movement (which requires another playing of the first movement) the two movements together form a single entity. A movement of this sort can appropriately be termed a *composite three-part form* (or *composite ternary*) and is found most commonly among the minuet and trio movements of the classical period as well as in the scherzo, which evolved from the minuet. Among such movements (in symphonies, string quartets, trios, sonatas, etc.) both the minuet and the trio are almost invariably cast as rounded binary forms. Scherzos, however, are usually more developmental in character and since they do not always follows the simple da capo pattern, are not all in composite three-part form.

RONDO FORM

Rondo form, based as it is upon the basic principle of unity through repetitions separated by contrasting sections, is closely related to three-part or ABA form. The term *rondo* and perhaps its structural principle may have evolved originally from the medieval poetic form of the *rondeau*, which contained repetitions of a couplet separated by longer sections of poetry. As a musical form it did not develop fully until the eighteenth century. It can readily be seen that by adding further repetitions of "A" to an ABA form and separating them by additional contrasting sections, the basic rondo pattern is formed.

Whether a rondo movement is diagrammed as ABABA or ABACA or has more than five sections, the basic pattern as found in rondos of the eighteenth and nineteenth centuries consists of literal or near-literal repetitions of an "A" theme—invariably in the tonic key—separated by contrasting sections in keys other than the tonic, and beginning and ending with the "A" theme. Although the term *refrain* has been applied to the "A" theme, it is more conventionally referred to as the *rondo theme*. The generally accepted label for the contrasting sections (Bs and Cs, etc.) is the term *episode*. (Some writers use the term *digression* in place of episode.)

During the classical period (when rondos were frequently used for final movements of concertos, symphonies, sonatas, string quartets, etc.) a characteristic rondo theme was a well-rounded entity in itself—very often a double period or a short binary or three-part form invariably ending with a perfect authentic cadence on the tonic. Usually in the major mode and with brisk tempi, rondo themes are often light and witty and with clear-cut phrase structures. There are, nevertheless, some strikingly beautiful rondos in minor keys, as well as slow movements cast in the rondo pattern. (The second and third movements of the Beethoven Piano Sonata, Op. 13 are cases in point.)

The final movement of J. S. Bach's E Major Violin Concerto is a fine example of a simple preclassical rondo. Its form, which can be diagrammed as ABACADAEA, is particularly clear because the rondo theme is always given to the tutti string section, while the episodes are played by the solo violin with a light accompaniment. Its sprightly rondo theme is typical in that it is a complete, harmonically closed double period of sixteen bars, in a fast tempo, and is light and simple in character.

Episodes function to add contrast to rondo movements—harmonic contrast by shifting to related keys or change of mode, melodic and rhythmic contrast by use of new thematic material, and contrast in sound by changed instrumentation, texture, or dynamics. Unlike the rondo theme, episodes usually are not harmonically closed and are often rather developmental in character, although there are episodes with clear period structures. In the simplest rondo movements, episodes may begin immediately after the authentic cadence which closes the rondo theme, but a transition from the rondo theme to the episode is more typical. At the end of each episode there is usually another transition (sometimes called the *retransition* to distinguish it from the transition which introduced the episode), which serves to prepare (usually with V) for a smooth return of the rondo theme. The composer's creative ingenuity is put to the test in these transitions, and classical composers often found strikingly beautiful or surprising ways to return to the rondo theme and to avoid monotony in its repetitions. Occasionally the rondo theme was varied in its repetitions—perhaps by altering the accompaniment figuration, as in the second movement of Beethoven's Piano Sonata, Op. 13—but its structure and key always remained the same.

Perhaps the most common kind of rondo in the classical period was a seven-part rondo diagrammed as ABACABA. Its form became sufficiently stylized in the late eighteenth and early nineteenth centuries that some valid generalizations regarding its tonal structure are possible. All of the statements of the rondo theme (the "A" sections) are of course in the tonic key. The first "B" episode is usually in the key of the dominant if the movement is in the major mode, and in III (relative major) or V if the movement is minor. The "C" section is usually the longest section, forming a substantial "keystone" or middle section of the arch. The "C" section might be in the tonic (parallel) minor if the movement is in a major key, or possibly in the key of VI (relative minor or major) or in IV. The "B" section, when it returns for the second time, is invariably cast in the home tonality, emphasizing the tonic as the movement nears its conclusion. The diagram in Figure 35 illustrates the typical tonal structure of the classical seven-part rondo.

	A	B	A	C	A	B'	A
Major Key	I	V	I	VI,IV or parallel minor	I	I	I
Minor Key	I	III or V	I	VI or IV	I	I	I

Figure 35

The above pattern will be referred to later in a discussion of the *sonata-rondo*, but first the sonata form itself must be covered in some detail.

SONATA FORM

So far in our discussion of structural stereotypes, of forms as labels, we have emphasized tonal or harmonic patterns. In looking back at period structure, binary, three-part, and rondo form, it should be apparent that all of these forms have one overriding similarity. That is, that all of them move from the tonic to the dominant (or some substitute for V such as III in minor) and then, through various more or less stylized tonal excursions, back to the tonic. It is hardly a remarkable observation, then, to note that sonata form does exactly the same thing. Given this fact, it seems obvious that a composer's uses of the stylized harmonic structures of the eighteenth and early nineteenth centuries does not tell us anything about his personal concept of the musical growth process. As Charles Rosen puts it in his book *The Classical Style* (W. W. Norton & Company Inc., 1972), "The movement to the dominant was part of musical grammar, not an element of form. Almost all music in the eighteenth century went to the dominant: before 1750 it was not something to be emphasized; afterward, it was something that the composer could take advantage of. This means that every eighteenth century listener expected the movement to the dominant in the sense that he would have been puzzled if he did not get it; it was a necessary condition of intelligibility."*

---

*From *The Classical Style* by Charles Rosen. Copyright © 1971 by Charles Rosen. Reprinted by permission of Viking Penguin, Inc.

But this is not to say that composers such as Haydn, Mozart, and Beethoven used the sonata form or other patterns simply as convenient, audience-accepted molds to contain their musical thought processes—that their only purpose in using the sonata pattern was to satisfy audiences who were prepared to accept only conventional patterns. Of course the real meaning of music can be related to thematic, harmonic, textural, and timbral phenomena and the intellectual or emotional responses that these evoke in the listener regardless of the "form" of the music. Nevertheless, the sonata form, particularly during the classical period, was a truly viable form for innovative musical expression, a pattern which could not be disdained by even the greatest among the classical composers. In fact, the sonata form was an ideal pattern with which to express dramatic and emotional feelings, the conflicts and "contraries" of the late eighteenth and early nineteenth centuries. The concept of two or more contrasting ideas or tonal areas presented in the exposition, the working out or elaboration of their conflicts in the development, and their resolution in the recapitulation—all of this forms a matrix of great dramatic potential. It was ideally suited to the dramatic characterization in Mozart's operas and the interplay of soloist and orchestra in his concertos. And it was equally useful to Haydn, Beethoven, and many composers of the romantic period.

In a sense, sonata form is a broad three-part form—exposition, development, and recapitulation—but it is clearly derived from the rounded binary form of the baroque. This derivation can be seen by comparing the diagram of sonata form in Figure 36 with the diagram of binary form in Figure 32.

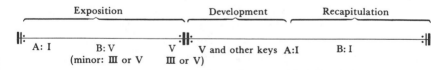

Figure 36: A Sonata Form in Its Simplest Pattern Showing Its Relationship to Binary Form

The recapitulation as seen in Figure 36 evolved from the *return* in rounded binary form. If the rounded binary form of the Vivaldi example in Figure 33 is compared with a simple early sonata form of the preclassical period such as Pergolesi's Trio Sonata No. 3 in G Major, it will be seen that the chief difference is found in the length and shape of the exposition and recapitulation. The basic binary pattern is clearly apparent in both movements, but note that the first section of the Vivaldi (to the repeat sign) is only seven measures long, while that of the Pergolesi is fourteen measures (there is no repeat sign in the Pergolesi). The features which mark the Pergolesi as a sonata form (or sonata allegro form) are (1) the presence of a second tonal group (and in this case a new theme) appearing in the first section in the dominant key at bar 7 and returning in the tonic key in the second section at bar 35, (2) the developmental character of the material at the beginning of the second section of the binary pattern, bar 15 through bar 30, and (3) the literal return of the main theme in the key of the tonic at measure 31.

Sonata movements following the basic pattern of the Pergolesi were written by many pre-classical and classical composers, for sonata form was the most important single movement instrumental form throughout the classical and romantic periods and continued to be used, though very freely, even in the twentieth century. One aspect of the form which remained constant throughout the eighteenth and nineteenth centuries is the pattern of key relationships. This is (1) an exposition which presents two main tonal areas of tonic and dominant (or I and III in minor) with a cadence in the key of the second tonal group (usually V or III), (2) a development section that opens in the key with which the exposition ended and goes through various keys in the elaboration of the thematic material of the exposition, concluding with a sizable section dwelling upon the dominant (called the dominant preparation or retransition), in preparation for (3) a recapitulation in which the material of the two main tonal sections of the exposition is presented in the tonic.

This is the basic pattern, but as sonata movements became longer, additional tonal areas were sometimes found in the exposition, slow introductions were frequently used, all of the sections were sometimes greatly expanded (particularly the development), and codas were added, often of considerable length. With all of these changes, the basic harmonic pattern remained substantially unchanged, even in nineteenth-century symphonies such as those of Brahms. In the twentieth century the basic principle of tonal contrast and return to a tonal center continued to be used in many sonata movements (the first movement of the Bartók Sixth String Quartet is an excellent example), although the tonic and dominant relationship was usually replaced by new harmonic idioms.

Much has been made by writers of the past concerning the themes and thematic relationships to be found in the exposition. Since there are usually two basic tonal groups, one in the tonic and a second in the dominant, the first has often erroneously been called the *main theme* and the second the *subsidiary theme*. This concept is incorrect on at least two counts. First of all, there is no evidence to support the idea that the second tonal group is "subsidiary" or in any way less important than the first. Indeed, the reverse is true in some sonata movements.

The concept of the two tonal groups as "themes" is also fallacious.

Frequently there are several themes in both sections, and sometimes there is nothing at all in the exposition that can properly be called a theme or melody. Also it sometimes happens, particularly in Haydn, that the thematic material of the first tonal group is very similar to that of the second, the primary contrast between the two being the shift in tonality. Occasionally, as in Beethoven's *Appassionata* sonata, the theme of the second group is a variant of the first.

The only fact about the thematic material of sonata form that applies generally to many sonata movements is that there are usually two or more contrasting tonal areas or groups in which thematic material is presented. The material between these sections must move to the contrasting key, and the term *transition* is correctly applied to these modulatory passages. As a corollary of *transition*, the term *retransition* has been applied to the section at the end of the development section which dwells on the dominant in preparation for the recapitulation. Perhaps a better term for this section might be *dominant preparation*. Another commonly used term in the sonata pattern is *codetta*, denoting the closing portion of a section of the form (other than the concluding section) which follows a preliminary cadence of that section. A *coda* is a substantial section following the cadence of the recapitulation, usually added for reasons of proportion.

The term *sonata* is, of course, also used as a generic term denoting an instrumental composition of three or four movements of which the first

First Movement:	Sonata form, sometimes with a slow introduction cadencing on the dominant. (The introduction is derived from the French overture.)
Second Movement:	Slow and lyrical, with various possible formal plans such as sonatina (a diminutive sonata form), theme and variations, or rondo. Usually in a key contrasting to that of the first movement such as the relative major or subdominant.
Third Movement:	Minuet and trio, often replaced by the scherzo in the romantic period. Usually in the same key as the first movement.
Fourth Movement:	Rondo, sonata form, sonata-rondo, or theme and variations. Same key as the first movement.

Figure 37

movement is usually a sonata form. The three-movement pattern, which evolved in the early eighteenth century from the Italian opera overture (*sinfonia*), was frequently used in the classical period for piano trios, violin sonatas, and sonatas for solo piano such as those of Haydn and Mozart. Johann Stamitz was one of the first to employ the four-movement pattern used in the symphonies and string quartets of Haydn, Mozart, Beethoven, and many other composers. This four-movement pattern evolved from the three-movement sonata or sinfonia of the early eighteenth century, which consisted of an allegro movement, a short slow movement, and a dance form such as a minuet. All that was needed to complete the conventional four-movement pattern was to add a fourth movement. The four-movement pattern then crystallized into a standard form as illustrated in Figure 37.

VARIANTS OF SONATA FORM

The *sonata-rondo*, common in late eighteenth-century music, is a rondo form which, for the most part, follows the basic structure of sonata form. Referring to Figure 35, note that the seven-section rondo pattern diagrammed there has a tonal structure that is similar though not identical to that of the sonata pattern. This is especially clear in the "B" section and its recurrence, which follow the same plan as the second tonal group of the exposition of a sonata form and its recurrence in the recapitulation. This trait in a rondo form plus a "C" section which has some of the traits of the development of a sonata form are the essential characteristics necessary for the movement to be labeled a sonata-rondo. Also, sonata-rondos may have introductions like those of sonata movements, as well as codas and expanded sections. One frequent distinction between a sonata-rondo and sonata form is that in sonata-rondo the end of the exposition (end of second "A") is often on the tonic rather than V or III as in sonata form.*

The sonata-rondo pattern occurs almost nowhere except as the last movement of three- and four-movement works of the late eighteenth and early nineteenth centuries (a few in this century). The form is found as the last movements of the two Beethoven violin and piano sonatas of Op. 12, the Op. 13 piano sonata, the Violin Concerto, Op. 61, the Eighth Symphony; as the last movement of several of Mozart's piano concertos and other works; as the finales of both of Brahms piano concertos; and as the final movement of works of many other composers, even in the twentieth century.

One of the most significant variants of the sonata pattern is the sonata

---

*The problem with this definition is that the exposition ends with a full close on the tonic rather than in the contrasting key as a sonata form should. Yet if one says, as do some analysts, that the exposition ends with the B section, then the development opens with a complete and unvaried statement of A, which is clearly uncharacteristic of development sections. Thus, the term "sonata rondo" is intrinsically problematical.

form as found in the classical concerto. It will be discussed in the next section.

Another variant of the sonata form is the sonatina or *sonatine*. As the diminutive form implies, this is a shorter, lighter, and easier version of the sonata form. Piano composers of the late eighteenth century such as Clementi and Kuhlau produced a number of movements in sonatina form as well as multi-movement piano works which used the title *sonatina*.

In general, aside from the fact that the sonatina form is a short movement, the most important feature which distinguishes it from the sonata is that the development is shorter and less significant in the total pattern, often nothing more than a transition (or retransition, as some writers would term it) through the dominant back to the tonic for the recapitulation. A number of slow movements of four-movement works of the classical period are also cast in this pattern.

CONCERTO PATTERNS

Among baroque concertos there are three basic types: (1) the *concerto grosso,* consisting of two contrasting groups of instruments (the *concertino* of two or more solo instruments against the *ripieno* or larger group of orchestral players, usually a string section), (2) the orchestral concerto, which utilized the concertato style but without the contrasting groups of instruments as in the concerto grosso, and (3) the solo concerto, consisting of one solo player, usually a violinist, contrasted to the ripieno. The distinctions between these three kinds of concertos are based upon the medium rather than upon style or form. Actually, at least after Torelli (1658-1709), all three types usually followed a three-movement pattern of a fast movement, a slow movement, and a fast final movement. The middle movement was usually lyrical in nature, and often followed a binary pattern. Many of the final movements followed a simple rondo pattern like the third movement of Bach's E Major Violin Concerto discussed earlier. The first movement, and occasionally the third, followed a flexible *ritornello* procedure based upon recurrences of a harmonically closed theme stated at the outset, separated by solo (concertino) sections of contrasting material. The procedure differs from the rondo pattern in that the recurrences of the ritornello were in various related keys rather than all in the tonic as in the rondo. The ritornello was typically cast in the tonic only at the beginning, at the end, and occasionally in its next-to-the-last statement.

The typical first movement of a baroque concerto grosso opens with the soloists and orchestra playing the ritornello material together, often in unison. In the course of this opening section a modulation is effected to a related key such as the relative major or minor, V, or IV. Then the soloists play contrasting material in the new key followed by another ritornello in a key other than the tonic. This is followed by a section for the soloists which modulates back to I in preparation for the final statement of the ritornello played by soloists and orchestra together. The form and tonal structure were flexible and additional sections could be added at the discretion of the composer.

Out of the baroque solo concerto gradually evolved the classical concerto for one soloist and orchestra. The three-movement pattern of the classical concerto was obviously derived from the baroque, the major formal difference being that the first movement was in a sonata form, modified to fit the needs of the new medium. The most popular solo instruments for the classical concerto were the piano, the violin, and the cello. A few were written for other instruments including clarinet, horn, and trumpet. Others, for groups of solo instruments, were after the baroque and pre-classical concertante models and were not true classical concertos. Mozart's *Sinfonia Concertante* for solo violin and viola with orchestra is an example of this last type.

Unlike the baroque concerto, the orchestra in the classical concerto such as those of Mozart functions on a symphonic level and the relationship between orchestra and soloists is that of two strong characters in a drama. The first-movement form shows this clearly, for the modifications to the conventional sonata-form pattern are those features necessary to create a dramatic vehicle for the two protagonists.

The main modifications are (1) the double exposition, (2) the use of trills at certain points in the solo part, and (3) the cadenza. Figure 38 presents

		Solo trill		Solo trill			Solo trill	
Exposition 1	Exposition 2		Development		Recapitulation	Cadenza		Coda
I	I V (III in minor)		V and other keys		I I I$_4^6$	V		I
Orchestra	Piano and Orch.		Piano and Orch.		Orch. (Piano)	Piano		Orch.

Figure 38: Sonata Form in the Classical Concerto

a diagram of the sonata form as found in the first movement of the classical concerto. The solo trill shown at the end of each of the main sections of the form invariably occurs on one of the tones (usually the fifth, occasionally the third of the triad) of the dominant of the prevailing key and is usually followed by an entrance of the orchestra on the tonic. The cadenza, or improvised embellishment of the final cadence of the movement, is derived historically as an elaboration of the resolution of I$_4^6$ to the dominant.

The classical concerto pattern continued to be used by composers of the romantic period, though very freely, and alterations in the basic shape began to occur almost immediately. Mendelssohn, in his Violin Concerto, abandoned the double exposition, let the trills be played by the orchestra, composed a cadenza which linked the development to the recapitulation, and connected the first and second movements by a single bassoon tone so that they were played without pause. Later composers, particularly Brahms, combined the scope and developmental qualities of the symphony with the virtuosic character of the concerto in compositions of four movements. Composers such as Liszt, Lalo, and Saint-Saëns sometimes abandoned the name *concerto* entirely, composing rhapsodic works which retained only the virtuosic solo part in dramatic conflict with the orchestra without the formal shape of the concerto. Twentieth-century composers continued the evolution process even to the point of composing works which used the entire orchestra comprised of groups of soloists without a lone virtuoso, as in the Bartók *Concerto for Orchestra*. Others, including Stravinsky, Hindemith, and Milhaud, reverted to the three-movement classical concerto pattern realized in their own individual styles.

VARIATION FORMS

The technique of variation can exist in practically any kind of music, regardless of form or style. Variation, like development, contributes to the growth process of music, but a distinction should be made between the two techniques. Variation is the process of changing or modifying a musical passage in such a way that the result is recognizable as having been derived from another passage, often retaining the length and general contour of the original. Development, on the other hand, is concerned less with the preservation of the identity of a musical idea than with the *gradual* unfolding or elaboration of its potential in the growth process of a work. A short motive, because of its incompleteness, lends itself well to development, for it can be transformed in such a way that its original identity is apparent only by tracing its elaboration throughout a piece of music. Variation technique, however, is generally applied to a longer passage rather than to a short motive, frequently to a musical idea that is already complete in itself. Figure 39 is an example of variation in very simple form. It consists of two phrases,

Figure 39: Chopin, Nocturne in F Minor

each of two bars, the second being a variation of the first. Note that all the tones of the original melody are present in the variation, altered by means of the triplet figure, and that the harmonic progressions of the two phrases are identical.

This is the type of variation technique most common in music of the seventeenth, eighteenth, and nineteenth centuries, and it is the technique upon which the classical *theme and variations* is based. When variation technique is applied to a short single theme to create a movement of substantial length, the result is called a *variation form*. There are a number of kinds of variation forms which have existed in the history of Western music other than the classical theme and variations.*

Viewing them chronologically, one of the earliest is found in the music of the Renaissance and baroque periods—sets of variations based upon secular songs, dances, and airs. In this type the technique was to decorate or embellish the theme with new figurations. This is like the technique illustrated in Figure 39 and in the classical theme and variations. Examples are found in the many lute transcriptions of *frottole*, in works such as the aria variations of Pachelbel, and in the works of many other Renaissance and baroque composers.

A second category is the Renaissance and baroque variations on plain songs and chorales. These are distinguished from the preceding type by a more serious and complex style utilizing contrapuntal devices, by the fact that they adhered closer to the theme, and that they were composed primarily for organ. Examples include *Salvator Mundi* of John Bull and *Von Himmel Hoch* of Bach.

Also in the baroque period is a third type which can be called the baroque ostinato variation. This includes the *passacaglia* and *chaconne* and the predecessors of these forms such as grounds, divisions, and those which were based upon famous themes such as the *Ruggiera*, *Romanesca*, and *La Folia*. Some of the best known examples of this type are the Bach *Passacaglia and Fugue in C Minor*, the Violin *Chaconne* (from the D Minor Solo Violin Suite), and the Corelli *La Folia Variations* for violin and continuo (Sonata No. 12). This type is based upon a short melodic phrase, usually in triple meter and four or eight bars long, which is used as a repeated bass line over which successive variations are built. Occasionally the bass line is omitted or placed in an upper voice for one or more of the variations. Some writers of the past have distinguished between the passacaglia and the chaconne by stating that the latter is built upon an eight-bar *harmonic* pattern rather than upon a

---

*A detailed discussion of the following categories of variation types may be found in *The Technique of Variation* by Robert U. Nelson (University of California Press, 1962). Nelson's nomenclature has been adopted here. Used by permission of the Regents of the University of California.

bass line as in the passacaglia. Although this distinction holds up for the Bach *Passacaglia and Fugue* and the Chaconne in D Minor, composers of the baroque period seem actually to have used the two titles indiscriminately.

Next in order chronologically is the type best represented by the classical theme and variations. It can be called the ornamental variation of the eighteenth and nineteenth centuries and is a successor to the earliest type discussed here, the Renaissance and baroque variations on secular tunes. Since both types aim for figural variation of the theme, the distinction between the two is primarily stylistic. The eighteenth- and nineteenth-century type is generally simpler than its earlier counterpart. The relationship between the theme and its variations is usually very clear, and contrapuntal complexity is avoided. The theme is invariably a complete, harmonically closed melody, often a double period or binary form; and the variations follow its form and harmonic pattern almost exactly. There are many examples in the chamber music, piano literature, and symphonies of Haydn, Mozart, and Beethoven. Schubert composed a number of variations using his own songs as the themes, including movements in the *Death and the Maiden* Quartet, and the *Trout* Quintet, both of which derived their titles from the songs used for the variation movements. Most of the variation movements in this category can be correctly termed *theme and variations*.

A category that is descended from the preceding type is the nineteenth-century character variation. It is, however, much more complex and elaborate than the eighteenth- and nineteenth-century ornamental variation. Its chief characteristic is that the separate variations each alter the character of the theme profoundly. The Beethoven *Diabelli Variations* is a good archetype and one of the earliest examples of the character variation. (The motivic structure of this work is also typical of the character variation.) The waltzlike nature of the Diabelli theme shifts to a slow majestic march in Variation 1 to a quietly animated style in Variation 2, and the subsequent variations all depart radically from the mood of the theme.

The nineteenth-century basso ostinato variation springs from the baroque ostinato variation, but differs from the earlier type in that it tends to be less homogeneous in texture and does not follow so consistently the principles of ostinato variation with its contrapuntal style. Thus, there is great variety of mood among the variations of a movement of this type, just as in the character variation. Most of the examples are for orchestra and two of the most famous are by Brahms—the Finale of the Fourth Symphony and the Finale of the *Variations of a Theme of Haydn*, Op. 56. The latter is particularly interesting in that the ostinato is five bars in length, in keeping with the five-bar phrases found in the original Haydn theme.

The final type to be discussed here is the free variation of the late nineteenth and early twentieth centuries. In this type the structure and harmonic pattern of the theme are often discarded in favor of free development of motives from the theme. Thus, the harmonic pattern and length of the variations often differ widely from the original theme. This type is strongly influenced by the character variation and includes works such as the Elgar *Enigma Variations*, the Franck *Variations Symphoniques*, and *Don Quixote* by Richard Strauss.

Of particular interest in analyzing variation forms are the harmonic and melodic relationships of the variations to the theme. The analyst should determine how the various musical elements are used in order to describe the specific variation techniques. Of interest in the growth process is the position of the different variations in the total time span of the work, their character change, textural contrast, etc., and how these factors contribute to the overall shape.

CONTRAPUNTAL WORKS

Obviously counterpoint and polyphony are used in virtually every kind of music to a greater or lesser degree. But there are certain kinds of complete works composed entirely or almost entirely in contrapuntal texture which have developed through the evolution of stylized procedures. All of them use imitation as a basic technique, and the most highly organized is the *fugue*; but there are a number of precursors of the fugue which should be mentioned before dealing in detail with fugal procedure.

A *strict canon* is a composition for two or more voices, maintaining the same number of voices throughout and using strict imitation throughout except perhaps at the end, where the voices may be adjusted to create a suitable cadence for the ending of the work. *Free canon* or *canonic style* is the use of imitation at the beginning of a passage, often in a work which maintains the same number of voices throughout, as in a Renaissance motet, but departing from imitation at some point following the initial imitative presentation of the musical idea in the various voices. Free canon or canonic style, because it is less restrictive, is far more prevalent in the literature of music than strict canon. Indeed, strict canons often sound very dry and academic. The Trio of the Haydn String Quartet in D Minor, Op. 76, No. 2 is a remarkable example of a successful strict canon.

The *ricercar*, closest ancestor of the fugue, began in the sixteenth century as an instrumental transcription of the motet and thus consisted of a series of sections in imitative style, each based upon a new thematic idea. Each section with its imitative opening can be called a *point of imitation*. In the seventeenth century the ricercar developed as a continuous imitative texture based upon only one theme. Figure 40 presents the opening of a Frescobaldi organ work, an example of the monothematic ricercar which, were it not for the tonal relationships of the entrances of the voices, could be called

Figure 40: Frescobaldi, *Fiori Musicali*, Opening of a Ricercar

a fugue. The concept of "answering," with the tonic and dominant relationship between entrances, is a later development which marks the beginning of the baroque fugue.

The most important type of contrapuntal work from the baroque period to the present is the fugue. Figure 41 presents the typical pattern of the baroque fugue as seen in a short complete four-voice fugue by Pachelbel. The development of the concept of tonality in the seventeenth century made possible the development of the basic procedure for the composition of fugues. Although fugue cannot be called a form, most fugues possess certain common

Figure 41: Pachelbel, Fughetta for the Magnificat

traits, many of which are illustrated in the Pachelbel example. These stylized fugal procedures can be seen in many of the great fugal works of Bach.

The traits common to most fugues composed in the eighteenth century are as follows: (1) A fugue is based primarily upon a short melodic idea called the subject. The counterpoint used against the subject in another voice, if it is used with some consistency in the course of the fugue, is called the countersubject and may also be an important thematic element. (2) Fugal texture consists of two or more voices. Although any of the voices may rest at certain points in the course of the fugue, the total number of voices remains constant throughout. (3) All of the voices are first presented in turn in the opening imitative exposition, their entrances usually alternating between the tonic and the dominant keys. (4) Fugal devices such as stretto, inversion, augmentation, and diminution may be used (though not necessarily) as devices for development of the exposition material. (5) In addition to incidental entries in related keys throughout the work, a final exposition or final statement of the subject in the tonic key is found near the end of the work.

Certain stylized features of the eighteenth-century fugue will be discussed in Chapter 7, including tonal and real answers, accompanied fugues, and exceptional procedures. Except for the tonic and dominant relationship between the subject and its answer in the exposition, most of the five features of fugue outlined above apply to fugues of the nineteenth and twentieth centuries as well as to those of the eighteenth century. Fugal writing is also used as a developmental technique in many works which are not fugues in themselves. Passages in fugal style, which may occur in a variation movement or the development section of a nineteenth-century sonata form, are often called *fugato* sections. It should be remembered that fugue is not a form but a procedure—some writers have termed it a texture. Every movement that professes to be a fugue has its own unique form, occasionally one that can be labeled as a stylized or stereotyped formal pattern. A case in point is the final movement of the Brahms E Minor Cello Sonata (Op. 38) which is clearly a fugue, with departures from strict fugal texture, but which is also a fully developed sonata form. This fact in itself, however, is of less interest to the style analyst than features such as the similarity of this Brahms fugal subject to the subject of one of the canons in the Bach *Art of Fugue*, the manner in which the musical elements contribute to the growth process of the work, the instrumental style, organic unity, repose versus tension, contrast, etc.

In this chapter we have briefly surveyed some of the chief formal patterns in use in Western music for the past three hundred years. There are, of course, other patterns which were also in use during this period, and there are also patterns which can be called hybrids or modifications of those discussed here. Musical phenomena such as cyclical forms, inter-movement relationships, unique multimovement patterns, etc. can best be dealt with in relation to specific works rather than abstractly. The abstract concepts discussed in this chapter will serve as points of departure in descriptive analysis.

SUGGESTED ASSIGNMENTS

1. Write an essay on the significance or insignificance of structural stereotypes in understanding the music of a specific composer of the eighteenth or nineteenth centuries.

2. In the literature of the baroque, classical, and early romantic periods, find and analyze the phrase structure of examples of simple binary, rounded binary, and three-part forms.

3. Discuss the evolution and use of rondo form from the baroque to the twentieth century in terms of specific pieces of music.

4. Write an essay comparing the form of a specific baroque rounded binary form with a sonata-allegro form of the early classical period.

5. Compare the relationship of ensemble to soloist in a Bach violin concerto with that of a Mozart violin concerto.

6. Find several examples of variation technique used in compositions which are not variation forms per se.

7. Find examples of the various types of variation forms from the Renaissance to the present.

8. Find and discuss examples of canon, fugue, and fugato in concertos, sonatas, chamber works, or symphonies of the eighteenth and nineteenth centuries.

5

Melody and Rhythm

Many writers on musical form have found it useful to separate melody and rhythm as two of the basic elements of music. It is true, of course, that rhythm exists in nonmelodic contexts. Rhythm articulates the meaning of purely harmonic passages, passages of percussion timbres in which no definite pitches are heard, and other passages in which melody, as such, is absent. But melody cannot exist without rhythm, for no musical series of pitches can exist without some kind of rhythmic shape. No matter how hard one may try, it is virtually impossible to sound a series of even two or three different pitches without their acquiring some sort of rhythmic articulation derived from durations, stresses, dynamics, or the profile of the pitches themselves.

Thus, to ignore rhythm and define melody as the shape or profile formed by any collection of pitches is quite fallacious, for no series of musical sounds can exist without rhythm. (This concept of the interdependence of the musical elements applies also to sound and will be discussed further in Chapter 8.) For purposes of analysis, however, there are times when the pitches of a melody must be considered separately from the other elements of music.

A melody, then, is a series of single tones which, because of its organization according to pitch and rhythm, conveys a musical meaning. (Obviously, the timbre and dynamics of a melody may also contribute to its musical meaning but, as components of the element of sound, they will be discussed in Chapter 8.) The traditions of Western music have led to one rather narrow viewpoint of melody as the "surface of the harmony." This concept could be applied only to music of common practice period and even there it would be most limiting. It should be remembered that melody is the only aspect of

71

music which in one form or another has been common to the music of all cultures and times. Furthermore, it is the one element most useful as a touchstone of artistic quality, for a composer without melodic ability is no composer at all. The analyst should strive for a broad, all-encompassing concept of melody, and an approach which can be applied with validity to the single lines of Gregorian chant, the polyphonic lines of Dunstable, the motivic structures of Beethoven, or the esoteric vocal lines of Penderecki.

Among the musical elements, melody is perhaps the most mysterious. Its ability to evoke strong emotional images, to create strangely beautiful states of mind hearkens back to music's primitive link with magic. Of course we don't consciously associate today's concert music with magic, but vestiges of early man's relationship to music can be found in our own responses to its affective qualities. A simple persistent rhythm, or two or three effectively placed tones of unique timbre can mysteriously evoke powerful images of strong emotion or great beauty in the listener. Our present-day reactions to music are often simultaneously primitive and sophisticated. They manifest our lineage with early man.

Melodies were first performed by the human voice, and because of this, they may bear a more direct relationship to the emotions than other musical elements. Perhaps this is why the powers of melody are so mysterious, and why melody is so difficult to handle in analysis. The analyst should consider the psychological or affective qualities of a melody. He should ask himself, "In what way is this melody beautiful, and why?" Within this context he should then determine how factors such as motivic structure, contour, density, scalar materials, and other aspects of a melody contribute to its qualities of musical beauty. And he should not be afraid to make value judgments—to say that a certain tune may be excessively repetetive, that its contour is unimaginative, or that it turns in on itself; to say that a song melody evokes a mood that is inappropriate to the text; that this melody is excessively stepwise, or that one too disjunct. One of the ultimate goals of style analysis is that of comparison and evaluation; and since melody is the central element in most musical textures, it is important to consider it from every possible point of view.

RANGE, TESSITURA, AND PROFILE

The range of a melody is the span of its pitches from the highest point to the lowest. A melody's tessitura is the general area in which most of its pitches are located, this area being viewed in relation to the pitch span of the instrument or voice for which the melody was written. Thus a bassoon melody which lies almost entirely above e^1* would be said to have a high tessitura, while an aria for soprano in which most of the notes are on the treble staff would be said to have a medium tessitura. Either of these examples, however, if written untransposed for flute, would be described as having a low tessitura.

When examining melody in works for large ensembles or even for groups of several instruments or voices, the range and tessitura should be viewed, for the most part, in terms of the individual instruments or voices, rather than in terms of the pitch span of the total ensemble. Also, when a melody is played by several instruments in various octaves simultaneously, the analyst must decide which of the doublings is preeminent for analytical purposes. A work for large orchestra will usually span the entire normal musical hearing range, so it is usually pointless to speak of range and tessitura except in terms of individual parts. A good illustration of this is found in the opening of Stravinsky's *Rite of Spring*. The opening bassoon melody should be described as having a high tessitura and a narrow range, both of which are important to its evocative qualities. Similarly, the opening melody for celli and basses of Schubert's Symphony in B Minor, "The Unfinished," should be described as having a low tessitura and a narrow range.

One of the qualities which contributes to the feeling of forward motion and growth in a short melody or in a complete work is the pattern of important points of arrival. These might be peaks or high points at various levels including the highest point, or they might be low points or valleys. The pattern of peaks and valleys in a melody is often carefully planned by the composer to give a sense of motion and direction to the music. A diagram of these points can be called the *pitch profile*. Figure 42, the rondo theme of the last movement of the Beethoven C Minor String Quartet, Op. 18, No. 4 has an interesting and purposeful pitch profile. If the analyst were to diagram the

---

*The following system will be used to identify the various octaves on the piano keyboard.

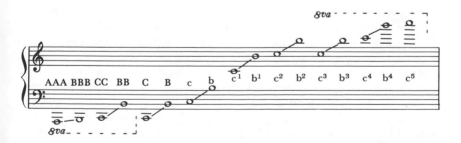

pitch profile of this double period, the B-flat in bar seven would stand out as the highest point of arrival. Then in the phrase which follows that high point (third phrase) the series of stepwise descending peaks (B-flat, A-flat, G) conveys a feeling of motion toward the half cadence at the end of the phrase. The fourth phrase, which is parallel to the second phrase, goes up only to A-flat as its high point, carefully staying just below the previously established high point of the melody.

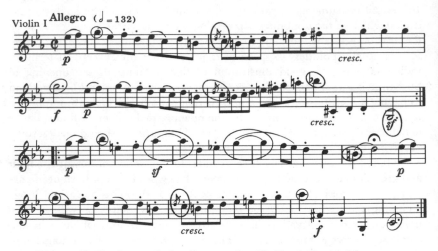

Figure 42: Beethoven, String Quartet, Op. 18, No. 4, Fourth Movement

The pattern that is drawn by the peaks and valleys of this melody might be clearly illustrated in a diagram, although often it is sufficient simply to circle the appropriate tones to show the peaks and valleys directly on the score, as has been done in the example.

Significant pitch profiles can also exist in such broad time spans as to be observable at the level of macroanalysis. For example, in the Brahms *Intermezzo*, Op. 119, No. 2, the note a^2 is the high point of the first section of the broad three-part form, and occurs only twice in that section. The second of these occurrences is very near the end of the section and clearly marks the climax of that section. Lesser peaks within the range of d-sharp^2 to f-sharp^2 occur throughout the section and seem to be deployed in such a way as to prepare for the high point at the end of the section. Then in the middle section, which achieves contrast by change of textures and a shift to the parallel key of E major, the highest point of the work, g-sharp^3, occurs twice in a time relationship very similar to that of the two high points in the first section. The final section reiterates literally the high points heard in the first section.

In a broader time span, the Prelude to *Tristan and Isolde* contains a series of steadily climbing peaks which finally culminate in the high A-flat heard three times at measures 81, 82, and 83 just prior to the denouement of the piece. In his First Symphony, Brahms seems to have carefully planned the arrangement of high points of each movement for maximum dramatic effect, saving the high c^4 for the coda of the finale. Careful coordination of peaks and valleys throughout a work can contribute much to the sense of musical motion and shape. Occasionally such patterns may appear to be unintentional on the part of the composer. The analyst's task, however, is not so much to determine the composer's intentions as to analyze the musical results.

In ensemble music, and particularly in works for large orchestra, the significant peaks and valleys cannot always be determined simply in terms of absolute pitches within the pitch span of a work. A piccolo tone, to use the extreme example, may not really have the effect of a peak because, in terms of the piccolo, that tone may be only in mid-register. Much depends upon tessitura in terms of the individual instruments, so that a cello passage with a high tessitura culminating in, say, the pitch g^2 may have the effect of a significant peak, even though it is much lower than other passages played by other instruments in the work. This is where the analyst must use ears as well as eyes to determine the real aural and musical effect.

SCALES AND INTERVALS

A scale is the pitch material forming the melodic (and usually harmonic) basis for a piece of music or a genre of music arranged in ascending or descending order according to pitch. Historically, scales were always determined after the fact of the music itself, usually from a large number of melodies written in a similar style. The most common scale in the history of Western culture is the familiar diatonic scale which furnished the pitch materials for much of the music composed during the common practice period. Even during that period, however, there were other scales in use in both folk music and concert music. The most obvious examples are the various forms of the minor scale, but there are also the chromatic scale, the whole-tone scale, the gypsy scale (c d e♭ f♯ g a♭ b c), and the pentatonic scale.

There were numerous attempts in the twentieth century to develop new scalar materials including the use of unusual scales from folk music (Bartók and Kodály) and the use of quarter tones and other intervals smaller than the diatonic half step (Haba and Partch). The twelve-tone system and other serial techniques do not, in themselves, form new scales, but the rows created by the use of these techniques do fall into the general category of scales. They differ from normal scales in that each serial composition will have its own unique scale (row) that is used for no other piece, and that the tones of the row (or its various forms) are to be used in an established sequence. Some twentieth-century composers have devised artificial scales by arranging half steps and whole steps in unconventional ways such as alternating the two intervals, placing a half step between every two whole steps, or other patterns.

In addition to the intervals formed by the adjacent pitches of the scales used in musical compositions, each melody also has another intervallic dimension. This can be described in a number of ways, but one important aspect of it is the measure of disjunct motion (leaps) in relation to conjunct (stepwise) motion. It is also important to observe the frequency of specific intervals and the size and direction (up or down) of the leaps. An actual count of the intervals larger than, say, a minor third in relation to those a minor third or smaller might be useful in analyzing melodies such as that shown in Figure 43. In this example it would also be important to note that every leap which follows a rest moves upward, which lends a climbing or aspiring quality to the melody.

Figure 43: Brahms, Sonata for Cello and Piano, Op. 99, First Movement

The intervallic and scalar materials in combination with the pitch profile, range, and tessitura together define the *contour* of a melody. Let us use the Brahms melody in Figure 43 to show how contour can be analyzed and described at the level of micro- and middle-analysis:

> Scalar materials in this case consist of the diatonic scale. The next step is to diagram the pitch profile as in Figure 44. The profile is complex, with many peaks and valleys, a result of the extremely disjunct nature of this melody. Because of this, there are nearly as many pitches in the profile diagram as in the melody itself. Range would be described as extremely wide, extending from c to g^2, and because of this the tessitura is both middle and high. The peaks and valleys, after a slight initial descent, show a marked upward pattern toward the high point at the

end of the phrase. This melody would be described as complex because of the relatively large number of melodic "bends" (changes of direction; the simplest tunes usually have only a few melodic bends.) The intervals are predominately disjunct, with many more ascending leaps than descending. Also, the ascending leaps are generally larger than the descending.

Figure 44

Many of these traits contribute to the sweeping, even aggressive, quality of nobility evoked by the melody. At the later stage of macroanalysis, the analyst should note that the high point of this opening phrase of the first movement is actually the high point of the cello part in the entire four-movement work.

So far we have limited ourselves, for the most part, to pitch aspects of melody. Rhythm also contributes much to a melody, to its evocative qualities as well as to the quality of motion. Motion or direction in a melody is derived from the nature of its contour and from a rhythmic factor called density, to which we shall now turn our attention.

DENSITY

At its simplest, density* is nothing more than the relative frequency of the occurrence of any sound in a melody or texture, and thus is a function of rhythm. Increasing the density increases the feeling of motion. A variety of density levels can be seen in the open melody of Hindemith's Second Piano Sonata in Figure 45. Examining only the melody itself in the right hand, note how the increased frequency of eighth notes adds to the quality of motion. The use of sixteenth notes in bars eight to ten increases the density, while the steady eighth notes in bars 10 and 11 in combination with the melodic contour effectively *move* toward the first important point of arrival, the high B in bar 13.

There are, of course, melodies in which there is little or no change in the density level, particularly in certain examples from the baroque. In such instances the feeling of motion is usually attributable to the contour alone rather than to a combination of contour and density. Figure 46 is a particularly interesting example of this because it furnishes the opportunity also to show several stylistic traits of Bach and of the baroque period.

---

*Another quite separate use of the term "density" is in reference to the "thickness" of a texture, though I prefer the term "mass" for this dimension.

Figure 45: Paul Hindemith, Sonata No. 2, First Movement © Copyright B. Schott's Soehne, Mainz, 1936, © renewed 1964

The two phrases of the chorale melody itself show, at a very simple level, how density controls motion. The only change in density occurs with the half notes at the ends of each of the phrases, which clearly tend to stop the motion at the cadences. In the organ chorale variation based upon the chorale, however, there is no change in density from start to finish, so that the feeling of motion is created entirely by the melodic arch (contour) of the two phrases. Since the melody in the right hand is in typical baroque "broken style," it is necessary for the analyst to extract the important high points or peaks of the melody from the continuous arpeggiated sixteenths. Except for the c's which occur at the beginnings of the first and second endings (4-3 suspensions), these peaks correspond exactly to the chorale melody upon which the example is based. Bach's variation technique in this instance is to arpeggiate each sonority within the span of the right hand, pointing up the tones of the chorale tune as the high points of each arpeggiated chord. The pitch profile, then, is almost identical to that of the chorale, but since there

O   Gott du from-mer Gott,   du Brunn-quell gu - ter   Ga - ben

Bach, Chorale: *O Gott du Frommer Gott* (2 phrases)

Chorale Variation: *O Gott du Frommer Gott* (2 phrases), Partita IV

Figure 46

is no change in density as in the chorale, the feeling of motion is dependent entirely upon the contour.

In vocal music the text in part controls the density and other aspects of the rhythmic character of a melody. That is, the natural speech rhythm of the words, the mood of the text, poetic meters, and rhyme schemes may suggest or in some cases dictate musical rhythms. Sometimes speech rhythms may transfer directly into musical rhythms without drastic alterations. This is almost always true in folk music, and this is why the folk music of a particular ethnic group will often reflect the characteristic rhythms of the language or dialect of that ethnic group. The Hungarian folk song settings of Bartók show this very clearly in that the rhythmic peculiarities of the Hungarian language appear in musical form in the songs. In Bartók's case this influence is also carried across into purely instrumental concert works such as the string quartets, so that the Hungarian language actually exerts a strong influence upon the composer's overall rhythmic style.

In art song and in various kinds of concert and church music for voice, there are often instances where the rhythm of the words is deliberately altered, sometimes by exaggerating a natural agogic accent or inflection so that the word still maintains its natural accents (such as lengthening an accented vowel sound), sometimes by actually changing or aborting the natural inflection of the word. It is not always esthetically desirable, then, for a composer to maintain speech rhythm at all costs. Indeed, certain composers who are noted for the excellence of the prosody in their vocal works, such as Henry Purcell, often take great liberties with the natural rhythm of the words in order to achieve the desired musical result. Only in recitative is the strict maintenance of speech rhythm the major objective, for here the communication of dramatic action to the audience takes precedence over purely musical considerations.

Figure 47 is an example of how a desired change in density took precedence over a natural speech rhythm without substantial damage to the poetry. First of all, it should be noted that the general mood of the song and many of its specific musical qualities are inspired by the literal meaning as well as the evocative qualities of the Heine text. The slow tempo, the low tessitura in both voice and piano, the slow harmonic rhythm, the somber quality of the accompaniment are all very much in keeping with the mood of quiet foreboding and dread evoked by the poetry. In a complete analysis, one would note that the motive B A♯ D C♯ heard in the first four measures of the piano part is developed throughout as a symbol of the ghostly double— the pale companion of the speaking poet represented by the voice. Of interest in this excerpt, however, is the fact that the poetically insignificant word *diesem* (this) in the ninth bar is assigned more melodic activity than any other word in the example. The result is that the density, and hence the motion, is increased at that point. One might argue that this is at odds with the ideals of Lieder, that Schubert here gave too much weight to a musical effect and not enough consideration to the poetry. Yet for some mysterious reason, perhaps because of the purely sonic qualities of the word *diesem*, this does not detract from the song, which seems, withal, to be an ideal welding of poetry and music.

Density changes can also occur in such a way as to be observable only at the level of macroanalysis. Perhaps the most famous instance of this is found in the slow movement of Beethoven's Fifth Symphony, in which the density

Figure 47: Schubert, "Der Doppelgänger"

level is markedly changed by means of variation technique for each recurrence of the main theme of the rondo form. Played by cellos and violas, it appears first in eighth notes and dotted rhythms, next in sixteenth notes, and next in thirty-second notes, with other varied recurrences appearing later. Variety within unity is thus achieved simply by changing the density. A similar unifying device is used by the contemporary American composer

George Crumb in the first movement of his *Night of the Four Moons* (1971). Figure 48 shows how three statements of a crucial phrase are varied in their recurrences throughout the short movement. Although there is a slight change in density between the first and the last statements, the important technique in this case is that of extension or development of a basic melodic idea. The example serves also to demonstrate a unique scale devised by the composer for a specific use. Thus, the common elements furnishing unity among the three excerpts in Figure 48 are the Lorca text, scalar materials (the same five pitch names and no others are used in all three fragments), contour, (the high and low points are identical for all three), and rhythm. Again, variety within unity.

Figure 48: Crumb, *Night of the Four Moons.* Excerpts from First Movement, "The Moon Is Dead, Dead." Copyright © 1971 by C. F. Peters Corporation, 373 Park Avenue South, New York 10016. Reprint permission granted by the publisher. Text: Federico Garcia Lorca, *Obras Completas.* Copyright © Herederos de Federico Garcia Lorca 1954. Reprinted by permission of New Directions Publishing Corporation.

MELODIC PULSE

One way to study the rhythm of a melody is to contrast or compare the rhythm of the meter to the rhythm of the music itself. The problem with this method is that meters very often shift, even when there is no actual notated meter change on the printed page. In twentieth-century music we have become accustomed to frequent changes of meter, and, as performers, we have learned to quickly adjust our inward pulse whenever the meter changes, even when such changes involve a change in the length of the pulse or beat or when the changes are very frequent. What we occasionally forget, as performers, is that we very often do the same thing in a work such as a Beethoven quartet or symphony, when no meter change is notated. Figure 49 is an excerpt from the first movement of Beethoven's Third Symphony, which is in ¾ meter.

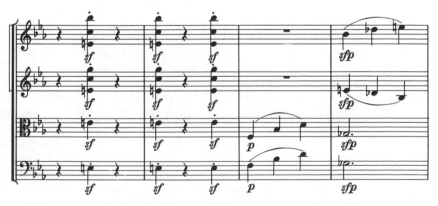

Figure 49: Beethoven, Symphony No. 3

In performing this passage most conductors will give a downbeat at the beginning of each measure; and this is quite as it should be, for the meter or pattern of bar lines serves the important function of keeping the performers together in good ensemble. But the passage is neither heard nor played in this manner, for the feeling of ¾ has been abandoned in favor of a shifting pulse which, if written by an early twentieth-century composer, might have been notated as shown in Figure 50.

Figure 50

Passages of this sort have been termed *rhythmic dissonances* because the rhythmic pattern of the notes is at odds with the notated meter, but in actuality there is no dissonance, because the ¾ meter has ceased to exist for a few moments, except on paper. The delight and interest of the passage is found in the contrast of the shifting pulse to the listener's *memory* of the steady ¾ pulse heard earlier, and the passage also lends greater meaning to the return to regular ¾ meter which follows. But this is not a rhythmic dissonance any more than a dominant triad followed by a tonic is a harmonic dissonance. A better use of the term *rhythmic dissonance* might be to describe the simultaneous occurrence of two differing rhythms in two discrete voice parts, but the term is unnecessary since we have the perfectly good word *counterpoint* to describe this phenomenon.

There are many times, of course, when a melody is set against a steady pulse played by another instrument or instruments. Indeed, this is probably the most common type of musical texture, described simply as melody and accompaniment. In such instances, musical interest can be generated by the contrast of the rhythm of the melody to the steady pulse heard in the accompaniment. But it is a rather dull piece in which nothing occurs in the accompaniment except the steady pulse of the meter. The contemporary American composer Kent Kennan's *Night Soliloquy* for flute solo with strings and piano is a piece which manages, because of a beautifully written part for the solo instrument, to overcome or at least minimize the drawback of an uneventful accompaniment.

If we agree that the pulse of a melody is the basic beat or meter that is sensed, felt, or heard as a background to the actual rhythmic pattern of the tones of the melody, then *syncopation* can be defined as a disturbance or contradiction of the pulse of the melody by the rhythm of the melody. Examples of conventional syncopation are very common in the music of the eighteenth and nineteenth centuries, the most frequent examples being those in which the beat is presented in the accompanying parts with syncopations occurring in the melody as, for example, ties across the bar line, etc. But what about passages in which the beat is not heard at all? Beethoven was perhaps the first composer to compose extended rhythmic patterns in which *all* of the parts were at odds with the rhythm of the beat so that the beat itself is not heard. Figure 49 is a typical example of this, but it should be noted that Beethoven generally placed this kind of passage in a context in which it could be contrasted to a previously established steady beat. Since all or nearly all of the music of the common practice period utilizes a steady duple or triple meter, it has been possible in the past to view passages such as the excerpt in Figure 49 as syncopations rather than shifts in the pulse of the melody. In the twentieth century, however, because of the vast amount of unmetered and polymetric music written since the time of Stravinsky's early ballets, listeners and musicians have been conditioned to frequent shifts in melodic pulse so

Figure 51: Bartók, *Mikrokosmos*, Vol. V, No. 133. Copyright 1940 by Hawkes & Son (London) Ltd.; Renewed 1967. Reprinted by permission of Boosey & Hawkes, Inc.

that many passages which might in the past have been viewed as syncopations are today recognized as irregularities in melodic pulse (i.e., as shifts in the beat). As evidence of the fact that there is disagreement on this terminology, however, Bartók used the title *Syncopation* for the example in Figure 51.

Actually, according to our previous definition, this should not be called syncopation, but rather polymeter with a pulse or beat of varying durations. In this case the accents are defined by the left hand and the eighth-note groupings. If we accept this as the logical indicator of the beat, the passage is built of groups of two and three eighth notes arranged in varying patterns. The melodic pulse or beat for the first two bars is shown in Figure 52. Additional rhythmic organization is found in the fact that throughout this excerpt, the $\frac{5}{4}$ and $\frac{4}{4}$ measures are alternated.

Figure 52

Figure 53: Beethoven, Sonata for Cello and Piano, Op. 69 (Scherzo)

An authentic syncopation is found in the Scherzo of the Beethoven Cello Sonata in A Major. As illustrated in Figure 53, the ties across the bar line in the cello part are clearly contrasted to the steady pulse of the piano playing the first beat of each measure. The steady beat, then, is actually sounded in this example—quite a different thing from the shift in melodic pulse in the examples of Figures 49 and 51.

Another important rhythmic phenomenon is found in the occurrence of two or more melodic lines of differing rhythms played simultaneously. Since this falls clearly into the realm of counterpoint, it will be discussed in a later chapter. Thus far we have considered rhythm only as it can be observed and described at the level of micro- and middle- analysis. As we shall see in the next section, there are important rhythmic factors to be considered at the level of macroanalysis as well.

MACRORHYTHM

Tension may be produced by any of the elements of music; and as discussed in Chapter 2, it is possible for one or more elements to contribute to tension (T) while the others may be contributing to the feeling of repose or composure (C). The balance of this so-called CT factor contributes much to the feeling of flux and movement in music. Rhythm, through variations in density and pulse, may often influence the CT factor. A unique example of this was observed earlier in this chapter in the discussion of the slow movement of Beethoven's Fifth Symphony. But there are other rhythmic features of this work which more clearly fall into the category of macrorhythmic phenomena. Perhaps the most obvious macrorhythmic feature is the recurrence of the famous four-note rhythm in varying forms throughout the work, from the opening tones of the first movement to the ending chords of the Finale. This could be described as recurrence, transformation, or development of a rhythmic motive. Another important macrorhythmic index is that of relative densities at various critical points throughout the work and how they contribute to motion and overall shape. This can be measured quite accurately by simply scanning the score. The analyst must bear in mind, however, that a relatively "black"-looking page in a slow movement may actually be of lesser density than a page of fewer notes in a fast movement. Thus, tempo is an important factor in mapping the density profile of a large work.

An overall density profile will frequently reveal points of extremely low density, many of which will correspond to cadence points. In most instances one or more of the other musical elements functions in combination with the rhythmic element to create the feeling of full or partial repose at cadences. In those rare instances when the harmonic element is not an important factor, the cadence is articulated or defined by the combination of the contour of the melody with the density level. This is simply another manifestion of the previously stated principle that density and contour control motion in melodic passages.

Ritards, accelerandos, and other rhythmic nuances are also of great importance at the macrorhythmic level. An analysis of the overall pattern of such nuances often may be helpful to the performer in determining the degree and quality of ritard, accelerando, or other nuances to apply at any given point—that is, how much and what kind of nuance to use. There are, of course, other factors to take into consideration in making such interpretive decisions. For example, a fast harmonic rhythm (which often coincides with a high density level) may indicate a ritard at the end of a large section, even if the composer has not marked it in the score. Contemporaneous notational practices must always be considered too. Baroque and Renaissance notation leaves much more to the choice of the performer than does the notation of twentieth-century composers. A performer of a Carter or Stravinsky work might well be taking undue license if he effects an unnotated ritard, but such practices are quite useful if not essential to the interpretation of much music of previous periods. Further aspects of rhythm as it relates to harmony and counterpoint will be discussed in the next two chapters.

SUGGESTED ASSIGNMENTS

1. Determine the range and tessitura and diagram the pitch profile for several instrumental and vocal melodies from various periods in music history.

2. Plot the pitch profiles for two or three complete movements of instrumental or vocal works.

3. Discuss several nineteenth- and twentieth-century melodies in relation to their scalar materials, balance of conjunct and disjunct motion, and the frequency of melodic bends.

4. Select an interesting melody and describe its *contour*, using the description of the contour of the Brahms melody in Figure 43 as a model.

5. Diagram the density changes for several melodies.

6. Select an appropriate vocal or instrumental melody and describe the manner in which contour and density contribute to movement or motion.

7. Produce a density profile of a complete work.

8. For a vocal work, show how the text controls the density profile and how it contributes to movement. Relate the discussion also to the contour of the melody.

9. Select a well-known composer of English (or other language if you know it well) vocal music, and evaluate his prosody in terms of two or three specific works.

10. Find and discuss several examples of polymeter and syncopation.

11. Find a contemporary composition in which both metered and unmetered passages occur and discuss their relationship to each other.

12. Write an essay discussing the macrorhythm of a classical symphony or chamber work.

6

Harmony and Rhythm

Harmony has been more thoroughly codified and systematized than any other element of music in Western culture. Indeed, harmony (along with counterpoint, which is a composite of harmony and other elements) is the only musical element which throughout history has been consistently treated as a theoretical subject for formal study. In the eighteenth and nineteenth centuries the study of *thorough-bass* (harmonization and figured bass realization) was the primary theory course for the beginning student of music. In the early twentieth century the course title in English-speaking countries changed to *harmony* without much change in content. Today theory courses in most schools still emphasize harmony and counterpoint to the near exclusion of the other musical elements. Where is the course in melody, the seminar on rhythm, the workshop on musical sound?

The answer isn't difficult. Formal courses in the other elements of music are almost nonexistent because the mysteries of melody, rhythm, and sound don't lend themselves well to the neat conceptualization that has been possible with harmony since the development of equal temperament, tonality, and functional harmony. So much of the harmony of the eighteenth and early nineteenth centuries can be neatly pigeonholed or labeled that it forms a sizable body of codified harmonic knowledge that can readily be taught under the heading "common practice." Most analytical systems, including that of Heinrich Schenker, emphasize harmony above the other elements, but such systems work well only with music of the common practice period because this was a time when harmonic practice had reached a stage of remarkable consistency. In a sense, it can be said that the system of functional harmony crystallized in the baroque period, and that by 1750 the diatonic-triadic system of tonal architecture (defined or controlled by the tonal center) had been brought to the pinnacle of its development—culminating in the music of J. S. Bach. *Crystallized* is perhaps the wrong word, for functional harmony carried the seeds of its own demise. Certainly musical architecture profited by the dominance of functional harmony and tonality, but expression lost; and even before 1750 many composers including Bach's own sons began to contribute to a gradual metamorphosis which led to the downfall of the system in the early years of the twentieth century. The diatonic scale was to music what the rule of the three unities was to drama—a sure means of organization, but a restrictive one—and the gradual erosion of diatonic harmony was the inevitable result of the need for greater musical expression.

From 1750 on the need for greater expression led to increasingly frequent and more distant modulations and greater use of chromaticism. In the eighteenth century this had begun in works such as C. P. E. Bach's *Abschied von meinem Silbermannischen Klaviere*, the introduction of Mozart's "Dissonant Quartet," and the Fantasia of Haydn's String Quartet, Op. 76, No. 6. In the nineteenth century it continued in numerous works of composers such as Schubert, Schumann, Liszt, and Chopin, finally arriving at a point of no return in late romantic works such as *Tristan and Isolde*. In much of Wagner's music, particularly *Tristan*, continuous modulation and abundant chromaticism made it virtually impossible for the musical form to be defined by tonal relations. In fact, though some theorists disagree, it has been argued that even the practice of beginning and ending in the same key became merely a vestige of common practice tradition rather than a working concept of tonal structure.*

By the end of the nineteenth century, the ear could accept virtually any combination of pitches in a sonority, provided that it was audibly derived from the diatonic tonal system; but even so it took a strong force to break with the well-established harmonic traditions of the eighteenth and nineteenth centuries. That force was found, most of all, in the ideas of Arnold Schoenberg; but even prior to the twelve-tone system, composers such as Satie, Ives, Debussy, Ravel, Scriabin, Stravinsky, and others were beginning to find new ways to organize harmony. All of these departed in various ways from the diatonic tonal system, usually without really making a complete break. For example, although the impressionist composers used many innovative harmonic devices (whole tone passages, planing, modality, root movement in thirds or tritones, eleventh and thirteenth chords, polychords), they did so without departing from triadic harmony. The twelve-tone system furnished composers with an entirely new method of organizing tones, relating them only to one another. Although many outstanding twentieth-century composers clung to certain aspects of diatonic harmony

---

*Anyone present when a symphony orchestra audience prematurely bursts into applause at the magnificent half cadence near the end of Tchaikovsky's Fifth (they often do) knows that modern audiences don't always hear tonal structure.

and tonality, the twelve-tone system was a powerful influence during the forties and fifties of this century. Today it is less influential; and in fact, harmony itself appears currently to be of lesser relative importance as an expressive element than previously. The elements of melody, rhythm, and, above all, sound seem to dominate the thinking of the progressive composers of today.

MICRO- AND MIDDLE-ANALYSIS OF HARMONY

Earlier it was said that the elements of melody, rhythm, and sound did not lend themselves well to the neat conceptualization possible with harmony in the music of the common practice period. It should be remembered, however, that those aspects of harmonic common practice which are easily codified are almost entirely in the realm of description. That is, having performed a thorough harmonic analysis of a classical work (labeling all sonorities with Roman numerals, finding all dissonant or nonharmonic tones, identifying all cadences, finding all primary and secondary key centers, etc.), the analyst really has done nothing more than thoroughly *describe* harmonic phenomena within the framework of the normative harmonic practices of the classical period. And having done this, what has really been learned about the role of harmony in the piece? Relatively little. The descriptive stage of harmonic analysis should be viewed as a process of data collection, and this data yields meaningful conclusions only when viewed in relation to all other data collected at the descriptive stage. Finding all the forms and transpositions of the row in a work by a twelve-tone composer yields similar results. Such data is meaningful only when viewed in relation to the phenomena of melody, rhythm, and sound within the total growth process of the work.

At the microanalytical level, descriptions of harmony center upon (1) the quality or type of sonorities used and (2) the relationship between a given sonority and other sonorities surrounding it. Certain aspects of the other elements, particularly texture, must often be considered in connection with harmonic analysis; thus it is virtually impossible to restrict discussion entirely to the element of harmony. Figure 54, an excerpt from an organ work of Mozart, illustrates a commonly used method of harmonic description in terms of Roman numerals, figured bass, and secondary V and VII relationships.

Numerals in parentheses represent implied chords or passing chords over pedal points. Melodic tones which are not part of the prevailing sonority (commonly called nonharmonic or dissonant tones) are circled. For additional description, terms such as *escape note* or *echapée* for the dissonances in bars four, five, and six; or *suspension* and *passing tone* for those in bar seven may be

Figure 54: Mozart, Fantasia in F Minor, for Organ, K. 608

used. This microanalysis might be carried further by identifying chord qualities (major and minor triads, qualities of seventh chords, etc.), though this becomes more significant in middle-analysis, when it may be found that relative numbers of various qualities of sonorities contribute to the CT factor, or to affective qualities. That is, a passage with large numbers of minor triads may create a certain mood, such as sadness or foreboding; large numbers of diminished sevenths may increase the harmonic tension; etc. One detail of chord quality relevant at this stage, however, is the fact that a diminished seventh occurs on the first beats of bars three, five, and six in the excerpt.

Middle-analysis of Figure 54 elicits the descriptive information that it is a period of two four-bar phrases, the first concluding with a half cadence, the second with an authentic cadence, both imperfect. The excerpt remains consistently in a four-part texture (with two small exceptions at the final cadence) with no voice crossing and in normal four-part vocal ranges. This fact, really a function of sound (texture) rather than harmony, is unremarkable from the stylistic standpoint other than to tell us that in this instance Mozart was adhering to the four-part texture derived from choral style which had been the norm since the Renaissance. It should also be noted that the excerpt begins and ends with triads with the third in the top voice (position of the third) and that triads in this position occur frequently throughout the excerpt. All four elements, of course, contribute to the hymn-like quality of the excerpt, as well as to other aspects of its overall beauty.

Since Figure 54 is a short excerpt, it cannot be considered from the point of view of macroanalysis, so let us now draw conclusions from the data collected in micro- and middle-analysis. First of all, it should be noted that the key of the piece, A-flat major, contributes an indefinable something to the evocative quality. This is very difficult to put into concrete terms, but slow movements in A-flat major do have something in common, as do fast movements in C minor, concerto allegros in D major, etc. There has been disagreement on this point. It has been argued, since standards of pitch level have changed over the centuries, that today we actually hear pieces written two centuries ago in a different (usually higher) key than that intended by the composer. It has been argued that the performer's concept of particular key is actually created by factors such as the "feel" of the key or tonal center on the keyboard or its appearance in the notation. Many musicians, however, tend toward an empirical acceptance of specific moods associated with specific keys, regardless of changes in pitch standards and other factors.

The prevalence of triads with the third on top is another factor which contributes to the affective qualities of the excerpt. This too, is hard to define. But for purposes of clarification, compare the excerpt in Figure 28 (slow movement of the Beethoven Sonata, Op. 13, *Pathétique*) with the Mozart excerpt in Figure 54. Both are slow movements, both are in the key of A-flat major, and both begin with the tonic triad in root position with the third on top. The similarity in mood between the opening bars of the two pieces is unmistakable, a fact which lends empirical support to the theory of specific affective qualities associated with specific keys, and that triads in position of the third (third on top) evoke a specific characteristic mood. There is more to be said on this subject, but to carry it further here would lead to a discussion of the phenomenology of musical sound that is beyond the scope of this book.

One of the most significant harmonic traits of the excerpt in Figure 53 is the use of the diminished seventh chords. The first one (VII^7/V with the C-flat borrowed from the parallel minor) occurs in bar three. Note that it lasts throughout the measure and progresses to a I_4^6 resolving to V with an ornamental resolution in the top voice. This ornamental resolution (consisting of a turn followed by an escape tone) occurs also in the following two bars on the resolutions of the diminished seventh chords occurring on the first beats. The harmonic and melodic sequence is obvious, but what may not be so clear is that Mozart's growth process in the second phrase is to develop the idea of the diminished seventh in bar three (and its resolution) at the beginning of the second phrase. Aurally, then, the first phrase generates the second, adding to the feeling of antecedent and consequent already apparent in the relationship of the cadences of the two phrases. The rhythmic and harmonic ambiguity of the first tone of the second phrase contributes to the feeling of motion as it resolves to the second beat of the fifth bar, and the same thing occurs immediately after as the sequence progresses. The repetitive (sequential) use of the diminished sevenths and the ornaments adds greatly to the organic unity (0) of the excerpt, but the repetitions are not dull because the harmonic tension ('T') is at its highest level during the sequence. In melodic analysis, we would note that the high level of tension is reinforced by the melodic contour, for the pitch profile would show that the melodic peak (f^2) of the period also occurs during the sequence. Harmonic tension is generally heightened in proportion to the number of chromatic tones (tones not found in the unaltered diatonic scale) that are present. Note that the first two bars of the second phrase contain four chromatic tones (A♮, G♭, D♮, and F♭). The feeling of repose (C) that is prepared in the seventh bar and achieved in the eighth is greatly enhanced by the harmonic and melodic tension created earlier in the phrase.

HARMONIC MACROANALYSIS

At the level of macroanalysis, the analyst should use conclusions drawn from micro- and middle-analysis to describe the general harmonic style. He should be concerned with harmonic unity and contrast, how harmony functions in the growth process, how it contributes to the tension-repose factor (CT) at the broadest level, how it adds to organic unity (0), and how it helps shape the work as a whole. For example, in macroanalysis of the Gesualdo five-part madrigal *Resta di darmi noia* (too lengthy to quote in its entirety), the analyst should be concerned with the harmonic sequence that occurs in the first eight bars (see Figure 55), the significance of the E-major and F-sharp major triads in close proximity, chromaticism, the harmonic implications of the various important points of arrival, and the manner in which the mood and meaning of the text are enhanced by the harmony. It must be remembered in a work of this type, which predates the common practice period, that, even though it begins and ends with a D-major triad, it is not "in the key of D" in the eighteenth-century sense. There is no doubt that Gesualdo and his contemporaries thought in terms of vertical sonorities as well as in horizontal lines. This is proven by the fact that in the text painting of madrigalism chord quality is often used to evoke poetic images (for example, the augmented triad on the word *death* in *The Silver Swan* of Gibbons). But the vertical thinking was in part controlled by horizontal lines cast in modes. Gesualdo's chromaticism stretches this concept to the breaking point and it is often difficult to relate his D-sharps and E-sharps in chromatic lines to the Renaissance concept of *musica ficta*. These unusual accidentals are often used as secondary leading tones to create what appear to be secondary dominant/tonic relationships. If the analyst accepts this theory, however, he may be tempted to inductively apply concepts of diatonic harmony to the work. This would be a mistaken premise, for the work was written before the establishment of tonal harmony (though it might be said that Gesualdo anticipated later practices).

Figure 55: Gesualdo, Madrigal,: *Resta di Darmi Noia*

Examination of Figure 55 reveals the sequence to be real enough. The passage from bar three to six is an exact transposition of bars one to three, and the F-sharp major triad in bar seven bears the same relation to bar six as the F-major triad in bar four bears to bar three. But are these true modulations? No, because without the firmly established concept of tonality which was yet to come when this madrigal was written, we do not really have a "key" from which to modulate. The modal feeling with D as the final is apparent (Dorian? Phrygian?), but this is not a tonic in the eighteenth-century sense. Indeed, in terms of eighteenth-century harmony, the D-major triads at the beginning and end sound rather like dominants. But eighteenth-century harmony really shouldn't enter into it. What we *can* say about this passage is that the F-sharp major triad on the word *pensier* is an important and (one would think) calculated point of arrival which will stand out in the listener's mind as an important event in listening to the whole madrigal. Perhaps the most important harmonic feature in a work of this type is the

	Exposition: First Tonal Group					
Duration:	5 bars (1–5)	5 bars (6–10)	6 bars (11–16)	7 bars (17–23)	7 bars (24–30)	5 bars (31–35)
Harmonic Outline:	I_____V	I____Mod. . .	II____Mod. . .	IV_____V	V_____V	I____Mod. . .
Key:	B Flat Major	C Minor	B Flat Major	G Minor	B Flat Major	C Minor

13 bars (36–48)	10 bars (49–58)	Second Tonal Group			
II____Mod. . . .I	_____I	22 bars (59–80)	4 bars (81–84)	6 bars (85–90)	21 bars (91–111)
F Major	A Major	I_____V	I____Mod. . . .I	____Mod. . . .V	____Mod. . . . . .
		F Major	F Minor	A Flat Major	F Major/Minor

Development (Mostly First Tonal Group Material)		(Mostly Second Tonal Group Material)		
20 bars (112–131)	7 bars (132–138)	5 bars (139–143)	2 bars (144–145)	6 bars (146–151)
I (Harmonically unstable) Mod. . .I	_____V	I_____I	Mod.	V_____I
B Flat Minor (D Flat, E Flat, F)	F Major	A Flat Major		E Major

9 bars (152–160)	14 bars (161–174)	17 bars (175–191)	5 bars (192–196)	6 bars (197–202)
Mod. V	I (unstable over F Ped) V	I____Mod.	I____Mod.	II____Mod. . . . . .
_____F	F Major/Minor	F Major	A Flat Minor	D Flat Major

7 bars (203–209)	1 bar (210)	Recapitulation: First Tonal Group			
I____Mod.	II I$_4^6$ V	5 bars (211–215)	5 bars (216–220)	9 bars (221–229)	4 bars (230–233)
E Flat Minor	B Flat Major	I_____V	I____Mod.	II__V__Mod. . . .	Sequential Mod. . . .
		B Flat Major	C Minor	B Flat Major	

10 bars (234–243)	Second Tonal Group			
I_____I	22 bars (244–265)	4 bars (266–269)	6 bars (270–275)	25 bars (276–300)
D Major	I_____V	I____Mod.	I____Mod. . . .	V_____II
	B Flat Major	B Flat Minor	D Flat Major	B Flat Major/Minor

6 bars (301–306)	4 bars (307–310)	6 bars (311–316)
I_____I	Modulation. . . V	I_____I
A Flat Major	_____B Flat Major	B Flat Major

Figure 56: Tonal Description of Trio in B-Flat Major, Op. 99, First Movement, by Schubert

manner in which the harmony evokes the meaning and *shape* of the poetry; but it would be a mistake to relate this harmonic shape to eighteenth-century tonal structure. (Here we are dealing only with harmony. Obviously, melody and rhythm also evoke images related to madrigalist poetry.)

In music of the common practice period, one way to approach harmonic macroanalysis is to describe the tonal structure by means of a diagram. Figure 56 is an example of such a diagram for the first movement of the Schubert B-Flat Major Trio, Opus 99. The diagram, of course, is not an end in itself, but a tool with which to draw conclusions about the harmonic and tonal structure of a composition. The exposition of this movement is shown in full score in Figure 57.

For example, the diagram shows that the overall tonal structure in terms of key centers for the various sections of the form is representative of the conventional practice for sonata forms of the late eighteenth and early nineteenth centuries. That is, the first tonal group of the exposition begins in the tonic, the second tonal group begins in the dominant, etc. More interesting, however, are the unconventional things that occur within these sections.

Let us look at one example. Schubert's great melodic gift is heard throughout this trio, and the melody with which the second tonal group opens (bar 59) is one of the composer's finest; but the overall beauty of its effect is derived in large part from the harmonic device used in approaching it. The key of F major is to be expected at the beginning of the second tonal group, but note that Schubert concludes the first tonal group with a strong emphasis on the A-major triad. The cello then takes the tone A, common to the F-major and A-major triads, and magically sustains it in space, as it were, for two bars. The second tonal group then simply begins on the tonic of F major without any dominant/tonic relationship. The breathtaking effect of the shift from the triad of A major to F major is enhanced by the sheer beauty of the melody, but the essence of the device is simply the shift from one major triad to another with roots separated by a major third. The same device is found at the second tonal group of the recapitulation (bar 244) with the first tonal group ending on D major and the second beginning in B-flat major. Note that in neither case is the conventional tonal structure of the sonata form altered—pointing up the fact that unique musical events are the essence of style. Similar progressions of the third occur elsewhere in this work and in many other compositions of Schubert—so often, indeed, that the "third relation" has come to be known as a hallmark of this composer's style. Another stylistic trait to be observed in the tonal description diagram is the multiplicity of secondary key centers, some of them distantly related to B-flat major, and the occasional tonal instability. There are no fewer than seven different key centers in the exposition, seven in the development, and at least six in the recapitulation. In addition there are at least

three places in the movement where the key center is so transitory or ambiguous as to defy definite analysis. In such instances the analyst should rely
on his listening powers rather than try to rationalize a key center. He should
be content to state that it is ambiguous, and to describe the ambiguity.

Figure 57: Schubert, Trio, Op. 99, First Movement (Exposition Only)

*Treble clef is used in place of tenor clef in early editions of some cello literature. When
this occurs, it should be read one octave lower, rather than as it is used in modern editions.
This type of usage is now very rare and can be discovered only by the nature of the context.

*Scholars and performers continue to disagree as to whether or not the sixteenth note in a context such as this (in music of this time) should be played as a triplet.

Figure 56 also furnishes a tool for the analyst to determine the methods by which the composer maintained the classical harmonic structure of sonata form. Note the frequency and placement of the sections in the key of B-flat major in the exposition and recapitulation, and the sections in F major (and minor) in the second tonal group of the exposition. One of the standard analytical procedures is to compare the tonal structure and relative lengths of sections of the recapitulation with the comparable features of the exposition. When differences are noted they should be explained. For example, why is the first tonal group of the recapitulation less than half the length of the first tonal group of the exposition? Does this have anything to do with the method by which Schubert arrived on A major at the end of the first tonal group of the exposition, and on D major at the comparable place in the recapitulation? How do the answers to these questions relate to the style of the late classical and early romantic periods, and how do they relate to Schubert's personal style? Of particular harmonic interest in this movement is the significance of the secondary key center of A-flat major—the structural importance of its recurrences and how preparation is made for the striking cadence on A-flat major at the fermata just preceding the final ten bars.

Macroanalysis, of course, can cover not only a complete movement, but also the composite of several movements which may comprise a total work. Approaches similar to those just discussed can be applied to the complete trio—all four movements of it. At this level the analyst should be concerned with the relationships and patterns of the keys of the various movements, the relationships of secondary key centers from movement to movement, the recurrence of unique or characteristic harmonic devices in the total work, how harmony functions in a broad overview of the CT factor, how it contributes to organic unity, and how it functions generally in the growth process of the total work. An important goal is to find harmonic features of the work which are typical of Schubert's style in other works; the harmonic features which are unique, even for Schubert; and finally how the harmonic practices in the work relate to the general harmonic practice of the period in which it was written.

As a demonstration of macroanalysis extending beyond a single movement, let us examine a portion of the second movement of the Trio (Figure 58). It is a slow movement of profound, elegaic lyricism, and much of its beauty is derived from the harmonic element. Although this is an early romantic work, in relation to the instrumental four-movement pattern of the classical period, its key of E-flat major (subdominant of the key of the total work) is quite conventional. But there its harmonic conventionality ends, for the secondary key relationships within the movement are truly remarkable. At bar 82 the first theme of the movement is presented by the violin in the key of A-flat major. Then, in bar 87 the minor IV chord in second inversion is used enharmonically to become VI in E major, and a striking modulation to a major third below is effected. The E-major section is substantial in length (bars 88-98) and is followed by another downward progression of a major third to the key of C major, which functions to swing the tonality back to E-flat major at bar 104.

Now, referring to the first movement, note the frequency and significance of the key of A-flat major in the total movement. Note also the similarity in melodic profile (contour) between the opening theme of the second tonal group of the first movement and the opening theme of the second movement—how both center around the third of the tonic triad and other similarities. Examination of the second tonal group material as it is presented in the development of the first movement will show its key structure to be very similar to that of the passage in the second movement from bars 82 to 97. All of this data can lead to some interesting conclusions to be drawn at the evaluation stage. For one thing, the modulations from A-flat to E to C and back to E-flat major reinforce our conclusion that the third relation is an important feature of Schubert's style. Indeed, there are many more instances of the third relation to be found in this work. At this point some other interesting questions should be arising in the analyst's mind which

Figure 58: Schubert, Trio, Op. 99, Excerpt from Slow Movement

*As in the first movement, treble clef in the cello part is to be read one octave lower.

also may be answerable at the evaluation stage: Does the emphasis on A-flat major in the first movement prepare for the key center and tonal structure of the second movement? If so, how? To what extent was this done consciously by the composer? What is the significance of parallels in harmonic structure between or among the various movements of the work? To what extent is harmony an expressive factor in Schubert's style? Assuming that Schubert contributed to the gradual demise of the diatonic tonal system, which was the stronger contributing factor in his style, chromaticism or modulation?

The opus 99 Trio is one of Schubert's finest and most significant works. Much can be learned about his style from this work alone. Yet for the analyst to draw valid stylistic conclusions and make sound comparative judgments, he must also have a good overall knowledge of Schubert's other works and of the general style of the period. This is one of the reasons why a good general knowledge of music literature and history is a requisite of intelligent style analysis.

HARMONIC ANALYSIS OF
TWENTIETH-CENTURY MUSIC

Certain harmonic concepts of the common practice period can be applied to analysis of some of the music of the twentieth century. This was illustrated in Chapter 1 in the brief discussion of the first movement of Bartóks String Quartet No. 6. (See the discussion of Figure 4 in Chapter 1 and Figure 14 in Chapter 3.) Examination of the score will reveal that Bartók's formal plan for the movement was clearly patterned after the classical sonata form. This being true, it follows that its form is defined partly in terms of its tonal structure. It is readily apparent that the work does not utilize conventional tonic/dominant relationships. How then is its tonal structure defined?

Although tonics and dominants are not used, the tones D and A do function to define the tonality of D. The melodic progression of A to D occurs frequently in the early measures of the work, most prominently in the unison passage in bars 15–18 and also as the first two tones of the main theme of the first tonal group (Vivace, bar 24). Note also that this theme (quoted in Figure 4) also ends on the tone A. D's are prominent and sustained in the first violin part in bars 28–31. These and other uses of the tones A and D in the early moments of this work firmly establish D as the tonal center or key of the total four-movement work. Because of this strong early establishment of a tonal center, the listener tends to relate all subsequent secondary tonal centers to the primary tonal center on D. Various methods are used in the establishment of these secondary tonal centers. At the opening of the second tonal group at bar 81 the theme in the first violin (also quoted in Figure 4) clearly outlines the dominant and tonic tones of the F tonality. In regard to style, the analyst should now be beginning to ask himself if perhaps the use of the first and fifth scale degrees to define tonal centers is a favorite device of Bartók. Further examination of this work and of other Bartók works would show this to be true. For example, the opening of the second movement of the Second String Quartet (Figure 24) finds the tonality of D defined by open fifths at the cadence.

The broad general principle utilized by Bartók in the examples just discussed is one which many twentieth-century composers have adopted. Simply stated, that principle is that the points of greatest consonance are often the points of greatest repose (cadences), and these points often define tonal centers. The question then arises as to how consonance (and dissonance) can be defined in twentieth-century music. Hindemith, in his *Craft of Musical Composition*, defines consonant intervals according to their location in the overtone series. Those lowest (nearest the fundamental) are the most consonant. The resultant order of consonance-degree is as follows: unison, octave, perfect fifth, perfect fourth, major third, minor sixth, minor third, major sixth, major second, minor seventh, minor second, major seventh, and tritone. Hindemith believed that the system was based on natural acoustical phenomena and thus was applicable to music of any period. And he attempted to use it (though not consistently and with varying degrees of success) in the composition of his own music.

The system possesses a few obvious shortcomings. For example, the tritone, which is cited as the most dissonant interval, is found in every dominant seventh chord. Yet the dominant seventh does not usually sound as dissonant as many chords which contain various combinations of minor seconds and major sevenths. Even so, the system can be quite useful in the analysis of twentieth-century music. It is even possible to devise a dissonance assessment system by assigning numbers according to Hindemith's dissonance scale to the various intervals present in a given sonority to determine its relative degree of dissonance. This type of dissonance quantification can be useful for comparative purposes.

Such a system should be used with great caution, however, partly because there are always too many unknown variables relating to consonance and dissonance, and partly because judgment of harmonic dissonance is a highly subjective matter. That which is dissonant in one harmonic context may be (relatively) consonant in another. The analyst's ear must bear the task of final assessment, for there is no system of harmonic analysis that can take into account all of the factors which contribute to the relative degrees of consonance and dissonance as experienced by the listener. The system is perhaps most useful in determining various degrees of dissonance in works in which the overall dissonance level is extremely high. A high dissonance level, of course, contributes to tension, and the analyst must remember that the other elements may also be contributing to the tension/ repose factor (CT).

Many twentieth-century compositions, non-serial as well as serial works, are written in a style in which the composer seems to be consciously avoiding any suggestion of triadic sonorities, functional or modal harmony, or traditional tonal structure. Often phrase structure will still be apparent, however, and it must rely on cadences. The analyst's task, then, is to identify the cadences, determine their relative significance in the total structure, their degree of consonance or dissonance, and other ways in which they affect the growth process and the form or shape of the work. In micro- and middle-analysis attempts should be made to identify frequently used chord forms (this term is used to distinguish sonorities which are not triad based) and intervals, and to relate them also to the growth process and to shape. Set and vector analysis of intervals can be very useful in descriptive analysis of serial music and certain other contemporary harmonic styles.

In the Milton Babbitt *Composition No. 1 for Piano* (from *Three Compositions for Piano*) the analyst should be able to identify a phrase structure based upon points of full or partial repose, to find frequently used sonorities or intervals (some of which are implied contrapuntally), and to plot an overall harmonic tension/repose profile which can be related to the shape of the movement. The harmonic element is inextricably linked with rhythm in this work, and this relationship will become very apparent by finding the various forms of the row.* It will become clear that the composer has divided each form of the row into two hexachords, and that frequently two different hexachords (from different forms or transpositions of the row) are overlapped to form a single rhythmic unit or phrase. (See Figure 59, the opening of the work.)

---

*Indeed, it appears that the *rhythms* (as well as the pitches) are more or less strictly serialized throughout this piece. See the brief discussion of total serialism on page 9.

There are various ways for composers to present the tone-row at the outset in its basic form, and this fact can make things a bit difficult for the analyst at the descriptive stage. For example, in the Babbitt work the analyst might have assumed that the basic row was presented in its entirety between the two voices in the first measure. If so, he would have concluded that the basic row was: B♭ E♭ F D C E A B A♭ F♯ D♭ G.

(possibly reversed)

Figure 59: Babbitt, *Three Compositions for Piano*, No. 1. Copyright Boelke—Bomart, Inc., Hillsdale, New York. Used by permission.

However, if this were the basic row, then the second measure should consist of one of the four forms of the row, possibly transposed. The analyst would soon have seen that the second measure was not one of the four forms of the row; at that point he should assume that he is in error and try another tack. If he then hypothesizes that each of the two voices presents a complete form of the row in their first twelve tones, respectively, he will find that the music satisfies the conditions of his hypothesis and that the original form of the basic row is presented in the lower voice against a transposition (in intervallic inversion) of the basic row in the upper voice.

Once the basic row is found, the analyst should extrapolate the other three forms and all possible transpositions. These forms with their annotational symbols are basic row O, inversion I, retrograde R, and retrograde inversion RI. A chart called the magic square is sometimes used as a reference tool in twelve-tone analysis. It consists of a square matrix with twelve units on a side with the forms of the row and its eleven transpositions filling in the 144 squares. Figure 60 shows the magic square for the Babbitt work.

The first step in constructing the magic square is to put the basic row in its original form across the top line. Then, starting from the upper left, put the inversion of the row down the extreme left column. Then complete the square by projecting transpositions of the basic row from left to right, using the tones in the extreme left column as the starting point for each transposition. To check your accuracy, see if the transposition of the basic row on the bottom line is an accurate transposition of the original form. Also check to see that a diagonal is formed from upper left to lower right by repetitions of the first tone of the original row (in this case, B-flat).

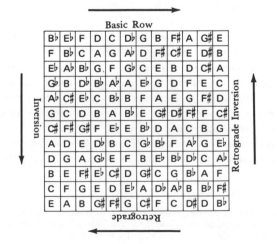

Figure 60: Magic Square for Composition No. 1 by Milton Babbitt

The names of the four forms of the row should be written exactly as shown in Figure 60. When reading the square, it should be turned so that the name of the desired form can be read right-side-up. The desired form and transposition can then be read horizontally from left to right. (Pitch names for R will be upside down; pitch names for I and RI will be lying on their side.) The magic square is a handy tool at the descriptive stage of twelve-tone analysis.

Phrase structures in serial works are often related to the serial structure. That is, one or more complete forms of the row or hexachord may be used to construct each phrase without overlap into the next phrase. This is not a requisite of serial composition, but it is true of the Dallapiccola example in Figure 24 as well as the Babbitt excerpt in Figure 59. Analysis of the serial aspects of the work, however, are actually less important than determining the phrase structure, harmonic usage, the CT factor, and ultimately the growth process and musical shape of the work as a whole. Analysis of the usage of the forms of the row is part of the descriptive stage and is useful in drawing subsequent conclusions about style, though it finally tells us more about the composer's compositional techniques than about his musical thought processes.

The example in Figure 61 from Ives' *Second Sonata for Violin and Piano* illustrates the manner of establishing a tonal center discussed earlier in connection with Bartók. E is very clearly the tonal center of the opening, and subsequent repetitions and pedal points on E leave no question but that E is the tonal center of the movement. Interestingly, Ives chose to conclude the movement not on E, but on a C-major triad, a fact which once again opens up the question as to whether the late nineteenth- and early twentieth-century practice of beginning and ending in the same tonal center or key was a significant element of musical shape or a meaningless vestige of common practice tradition.

From the standpoint of harmonic style, the work shows Ives to be a daring innovator. The chord forms, though derived from triads, are unique for having been composed during the early years of this century. The whole-tone implications of the first bar* are not so remarkable in light of the Impressionists' and the Russians' use of whole-tone harmonies. More worthy of note is the fact that the first measure contains all of the tones of one of the two whole-tone scales, and no other tones. Note also that the sonority on the second beat of the second bar is a polychord consisting of an augmented triad and a major triad. The phrase structure confirms the tonal

---

*Ives sometimes omitted conventional bar lines to minimize the "metered" feeling of the music for greater rhythmic freedom and flow. The dotted bar lines aid the performers even though the number of beats varies from measure to measure.

Figure 61: Ives, Second Sonata for Violin and Piano, Third Movement ("The Revival"). Copyright Associated Music Publishers. Used by permission.

center of E, for the first phrase (concluding at the end of bar four) begins and ends on E. The growth process at the beginning of the second bar relies upon the repetition (with variation) of the basic harmony with which the first phrase ended. Another instance of harmonic simultaneity occurs in the second phrase at the *piu mosso* in the piano part, where both whole-tone scales are presented simultaneously in upward scalar progression, one in the left hand, the other in the right. This is consistent with the harmonic materials heard at the beginning and elsewhere in the excerpt—harmony contributing to organic unity.

Another twentieth-century development is the use of electronic sounds. In Chapter 1 it was mentioned that compositions which combine instruments or voices with electronic sounds are easier to analyze than pure electronic works. One of the main reasons for this is that the presence of the human performer makes it necessary for the composer to at least partially notate the electronic sounds in order to furnish the performers with cues for synchronization. Thus, the score contains not only the accurate notation for the singers or instrumentalists, but also partial notation, in some cases quite specific, for the electronic sounds. *Synchronisms No. 3 for Cello and Electronic Sounds* (1964) by Mario Davidovsky is a good example.* The cello part is notated in full, and in addition, each of the entrances and endings of the tape is shown. Also, wherever the performer might have difficulty synchronizing with the electronic sounds, the composer has indicated the specific pitches and rhythms (though not timbres) of the electronic sounds in more or less conventional notation. In illustration of this, an excerpt from the work is shown in Figure 62.

Figure 62: Davidovsky, *Synchronisms No. 3 for Cello and Electronic Sounds.* ©Copyright McGinnis & Marx, New York. Used by permission.

Obviously, when the notation is this complete, the analyst can approach the work in the usual manner. However, in the many sections of the work where little or nothing of the electronic sound is notated, the analyst must refer to a recording of the work and rely on his ears. In analysis of any electronic work it is important to listen to a recording of the work repeatedly in order to be sure of the specific timbres, pitches, and rhythms. Only by this means can an accurate assessment of the organic unity, growth process, and originality be made. In the case of the Davidovsky work, frequently used chord forms, intervals, and rhythms can be found not only in the cello part but also in the electronic part. A case can even by made for a tonality of E (though the work ends ambiguously), for in addition to the long opening E in the cello part, there are frequent and prominent uses of B and E throughout the work plus a long E pedal point at the end of the third tape segment. In the past two decades electronics has created an important new source of musical material. The works which comprise this new body of literature

---

*The author was privileged to perform the world première of this piece early in 1965.

should be appraised from the stylistic point of view in much the same way as works for conventional instruments and voices.

There are many composers of today who have experimented very little or not at all with electronic music. Others have used electronic sounds only occasionally. A considerable number have devoted themselves almost exclusively to it. The electronic composers in the last category are divided into two basic camps. The first category consists of those who work in a so-called classical studios with a dozen or more signal generators, several tape decks (for splicing, replaying, modification, etc.), white noise generator, envelope control, patch board or mixer, and various peripheral pieces of equipment. The second category consists of those who concentrate on the use of various kinds of synthesizers, both for improvisation in performance and for composition, thus avoiding the extensive and painstaking splicing process practiced in the classical studio. In this last category are works which are partially or totally improvisatory in nature. Though they may have great artistic value, it is pointless to attempt to analyze such works, for their existence is ephemeral—each subsequent performance is a new musical experience.

Electronic works of all kinds have collectively brought about one specific effect on the musical environment of our time—they have expanded the aural horizons of composers and listeners. This is perhaps most apparent among composers who have had little to do with electronics in their own music. There are new sounds to be heard in electronic music, and these sounds have unlocked hidden and unsuspected sources for new sounds in music for conventional instruments and voices. Thus, the creative mind of the non-electronic composer has been renewed with a wealth of striking new possibilities that might not have come to him had he not been exposed to the rich diversity of texture and timbre in electronic music.

SETS AND INTERVAL VECTORS

Obviously, in approaching recent twentieth century music the analyst will often be confronted with the problem of describing harmonies which are non-triadic in nature—sonorities for which the terminology often applied to common practice music is useless. Set theory can be very useful for such music; and it should be part of the equipment of every musician who approaches twentieth century music. A *set* (as applied to music) is a group of tones sounded together (a chord) or several separate tones in close proximity heard as a group (that is, that they have the same harmonic implications as a chord). The interval vector tells how many intervals of each interval classification are found in the set. A table of the interval classifications is shown on page 120:

Interval Class	Intervals	Mod-12
I	m2-M7	1-11
II	M2-m7	2-10
III	m3-M6	3-9
IV	M3-m6	4-8
V	P4-P5	5-7
VI	tritone	6

The Mod-12 column at the extreme right refers to the number of half steps found in each of the intervals. Based on the interval class system, the interval vector is a simple device for determining and communicating harmonic quality on the basis of intervallic content.

One starts with a chord or several tones that are grouped together in the context of the music, such as:

Figure 63: A group of tones extracted from a musical context for which the analyst wishes to determine the intervallic content.

This group of tones is then converted to what is called "normal order" by rearranging them in ascending order within the smallest intervallic span, like this:

Figure 64: Normal order for the pitches presented in Fig. 63.

Obviously, normal order utilizes octave displacement to reduce all pitches to within an octave. Pitch class, then, rather than real pitch, is characteristic of the system, just as in Schenkerian analysis. Next, the lowest pitch in the normal order is represented by zero while the other pitches are

assigned numbers representing the number of half steps by which each of
them is separated from the lowest pitch, as follows:

0   1   5   6   7

Figure 65: Pitch-Set

The resulting row of numbers (0, 1, 5, 6, 7) is called the pitch-set.
The mod-12 system discussed above has been used to arrive at (0, 1, 5, 6,
7). This pitch-set can be thought of as a kind of tag or label for that group
of pitches. Indeed, as the analyst gains experience in set theory, he or she
will begin to refer to sonorities in twentieth century music in terms of their
pitch-sets. Pitch-sets describe the relationship of each tone in the sonority
to the lowest tone (in normal order); but pitch-sets do not describe the
intervallic content of a group of pitches.

To do that, the analyst must construct an interval vector. An interval
vector is a six-digit display with each digit from I through VI representing
the six interval classes, respectively. The number that appears in each of
the six places indicates the number of intervals of each interval class to be
found in the set. The first step in building the vector is to construct a
"subtraction triangle." The set we arrived at above is placed across the top
as follows:

$$0 \quad 1 \quad 5 \quad 6 \quad 7$$
$$4 \quad 5 \quad 6$$
$$1 \quad 2$$
$$1$$

To get the second row of numbers we take the first number (other than
"0") and subtract it from each of the other numbers in the set—1 from 5,
1 from 6, and 1 from 7, thus arriving at 4-5-6 in the second row. The same
is done for each subsequent row, working downward to one digit. Then using
the Mod-12 column from the interval class table, we count the number of
digits representing each interval class and place those totals in the six places
of the interval vector. Of "1's" and "11's" in the subtraction triangle there
are three; so we put the number "3" in the first place of the interval vector.
Of "2's" and "10's" there is only one; so one goes in the second place. There
are no "3's" or "9's"; one "4" (no "8's"); of "5's" and "7's" there are three;

and there are two "6's." This produces the following interval vector:

$$3 \quad 1 \quad 0 \quad 1 \quad 3 \quad 2$$

With a little experience one learns to "read" the interval vector to observe that, while there are no third-class intervals (m3-M6), there are three each of first and fifth classes, meaning that the predominant intervals in the pitch-set are perfect intervals (P4-P5) and the highly dissonant half steps (or major sevenths). That there are two tritones adds to the dissonance, and the remaining intervals are one whole step and one major third.

The purpose here is to understand how to produce an interval vec-tor—a systematic approach to determine the intervallic content of any collec-tion of pitches. The system is most appropriate for non-triadic sonorities of the sort that appear in much twentieth century music. After all, we already have well understood vocabularies for describing functional triadic music and other musics of the past. Intervallic content can be heard, of course, and the analyst should rely upon aural perception. Interval vectors, however, can lead the analyst toward stylistic conclusions, or can confirm hypotheses. If a number of interval vectors in a certain composition are found to be rich in perfect intervals and minor seconds, this may be an important factor for the analyst to observe. It should also be pointed out that one can often scan a simple sonority (such as a three-tone sonority) to determine its intervallic content without resorting to the interval vector. The interval vector should be viewed as a shortcut to determine intervallic content in complex twentieth century sonorities.

There is also a simple formula, well known to statisticians, by which one can check for accuracy. It simply tells you the number of possible pairs in any collection of elements. Pairs, in this case means intervals, and "n" represents the number of tones in the original pitch-set.

$$\frac{n^2 - n}{2} \quad = \text{(total of the numbers in the vector)}$$

$$\frac{25 - 5}{2} \quad = 10$$

$$10 \quad = 10$$

What the formula says is that 10 is the total number of possible intervals in a five tone set and that should equal the number of intervals represented in the vector.

This approach to analysis was first set forth by Howard Hanson in *The Harmonic Materials of Modern Music* (New York: Appleton-Century-Crofts, 1960) as a method by which composers could more fully comprehend the harmonic properties of twentieth-century music. His system used letters to represent the six interval classes, but a few years later Allen Forte pres-ented a numerical version of the system in an article entitled "A Theory of Set Complexes for Music" (*JMT* 8, 1964: 136-183). Then in Forte's *The Structure of Atonal Music* (New Haven and London: Yale University Press, 1973) he presented the approach to interval vectors that has been described here. The letters of Hanson's system may be just as usable as the numerals, but since the latter are in more common use today, it is the numerical version that I have presented here.

The system is most often used as an analytical tool, and the critical step is the initial selection of the pitch-sets that are to furnish the basis for analysis. The rule-of-thumb is to group pitches together if, in one way or another, they are heard together as a discrete musical unit—as a harmonic entity. Vertical sonorities (chords) form pitch-sets in themselves; but linear pitches, if together they possess the harmonic implications of a chord, can also form pitch-sets, as can combinations of vertical and linear pitches. Phrase and dynamic markings may delineate pitch-sets, and the element of sound as manifest in the instrumentation may also be a factor.

An interesting phenomenon of interval vectors is the fact that the mirror inversion of a sonority will have the same interval vector as the sonority itself. Thus a major triad and a minor triad will have the same interval vector as will a half-diminished seventh and a major-minor seventh. This is a controversial issue from the perspective of the phenomenology of musical sound as well as in regard to the validity of interval vectors in the analysis of music. Since it is perhaps beside the point here, and because I have discussed this issue elsewhere* it seems inappropriate to carry it further. Suffice it to say that the mathematical study and manipulation of pitch-sets and interval vectors has become an active area of scholarship in contemporary theory.

HARMONIC RHYTHM

Harmonic rhythm is the rhythmic profile formed by the changes in harmony in the course of a piece of music. It is often referred to as the relative speed with which the harmonies change. That is, a Bach chorale may be said to have a fast harmonic rhythm because there is a change of chord on each beat, while the opening of Mendelssohn's "Italian Symphony" would be described as a slow harmonic rhythm because the A major triad is continued over several measures, and the subsequent chord changes are relatively infrequent. But there is more to harmonic rhythm than simply the relative frequency of chord changes.

In the music of the common practice period certain chord progressions possess strong rhythmic implications which may or may not coincide with

---

Guidelines for College Teaching of Music Theory (Metuchen, N.J.: Scarecrow Press, 1981), pp. 60-62.

the rhythm of the meter. For example, the progression of dominant to tonic will often create the impression of weak to strong or of short to long. Composers, however, may wish to deliberately change this natural implication by placing the "weak" part of the progression on a strong beat, shortening the duration of the "strong" chord, using dynamics which are at odds with the normal feeling of strong and weak, or other devices. Such practices are stylistically interesting to the analyst, for music adhering strictly to the implications of harmonic rhythm would be quite dull.

The pattern of harmonic change often will coincide with the rhythm of the meter. That is, chord changes may occur on strong beats of the meter with a degree of regularity. At other times the profile of harmonic change may be quite independent of both the melodic pulse and the meter. The excerpt from the Beethoven piano sonata Op. 31, No. 3 shown in Figure 63 is a good example of this. Although there is a tonic harmony at the beginning of each bar, the rhythmic pattern of chord changes appears to be independent of the rhythms of the melodic lines. This example also demonstrates the implications that harmonic rhythm may have for performance. Note the gradual increase in the speed of the harmonic rhythm as the phrase nears its cadence, a phenomenon which often calls for a nuance such as a slight ritard.

At the level of macroanalysis, it may be found in a large work that the composer has used harmonic rhythm as a factor of shape and contrast. For example, in the first movement of the Beethoven piano sonata Op. 27, No. 2, the harmonic rhythm is relatively slow, in keeping with the prevailing mood of serenity, often with a single sonority lasting for one complete

Figure 66: Beethoven, Piano Sonata, Op. 31, No. 3. Pattern of Harmonic Rhythm

measure. In the second movement (Allegretto) there is a chord change on nearly every beat of the first section, contrasted to a somewhat slower harmonic rhythm in the Trio. The Finale then returns to a slow harmonic rhythm but in a fast energetic tempo to conclude the work in a spirited mood. The work begins and ends, then, in a slow harmonic rhythm, with contrast in the middle sections. In fact, with the trio of the da capo middle movement as the keystone, the harmonic rhythm profile forms a symmetrical arch.

Twentieth-century composers are perhaps less aware of harmonic rhythm as an expressive factor than were their predecessors in the common practice period. This is partly due to the gradual disappearance of functional harmony. In its place rhythmic interest is achieved by increased rhythmic and contrapuntal complexity, frequent changes of meter, asymmetrical meters, and other rhythmic devices.

SUGGESTED ASSIGNMENTS

1. Perform a detailed harmonic microanalysis of a brief movement from a classical piano sonata.

2. Perform a middle-analysis of the work studied in assignment number 1 and draw conclusions about its affective qualities and the growth process based on its form, the CT factor, chord qualities, harmonic progressions, harmonic rhythm, and other factors relating to harmony.

3. Repeat the process of the preceding assignments on a brief twelve-tone work, first finding all the forms and transpositions of the row.

4. Consider the two works studied in the preceding assignments from the standpoint of macroanalysis, commenting on the CT factor, harmonic unity and contrast, the growth process as it relates to harmony, and organic unity.

5. Make a tonal diagram (as in Figure 56) of a substantial movement of a nineteenth-century chamber work. Draw conclusions about harmonic style based on the diagram.

6. Perform a macroanalysis of the complete Schubert Trio (Op. 99) discussed in this chapter.

7. Discuss the ways in which the four movements of Bartók's Sixth String Quartet are harmonically and melodically related.

8. Discuss tonal centers in another Bartók chamber work (or other early twentieth-century composition).

9. Using Hindemith's ordering of consonance-degree (as well as your ears), plot a harmonic CT profile of a piano movement of Hindemith. Relate this profile to the CT factor observed in relation to the other elements.

10. Diagram the phrase structure of a twelve-tone work, and discuss the relationship of the structure to the use of the row.

11. Find and discuss examples of harmonic simultaneity in several twentieth-century compositions.

12. Attempt to describe the tonal or harmonic structure of a work for electronic sounds in combination with voices or instruments.

13. Diagram the harmonic rhythm profile of a complete classical sonata.

14. For a short contemporary work of your own choosing, select several sonorities that are highly characteristic of the composition and find their interval vectors. From the nature of the vectors, draw some conclusions about the composer's harmonic style.

7

Counterpoint

A contrapuntal texture is the composite musical effect produced by the juxtaposition of pitch and rhythm between two or more voice lines. In studying a contrapuntal texture, the analyst should be concerned with the factors found in any piece of music, that is, the growth process, the CT factor, shape, how all of the elements function in toto, etc. But in addition, counterpoint should be examined from the point of view of one very specific aspect of historical style: the attitude toward consonance and dissonance in relation to rhythm in the various periods of music history. Ideally, the analyst should himself be a skilled contrapuntist and should have a broad knowledge of contrapuntal practices and theoretical writings from the time of Guido's *Micrologus* to twentieth-century serial composition. But the pool of information on this subject is so vast that few musicians, even if skilled in counterpoint, could hope to have this body of knowledge at their fingertips. In the seventeenth century alone there were literally thousands of theoretical treatises written by amateur and professional musicians and scholars in Europe and the British Isles. Since most musicians, composers excepted, are not skilled contrapuntists, it is understandable that they will approach contrapuntal analysis with a synoptic view of the major changes in contrapuntal practice from the Middle Ages to the present rather than with a practical comprehensive knowledge. Most musicians have some familiarity with counterpoint since the Renaissance, but it is important for the analyst also to be familiar at least with the major changes in contrapuntal practice in the period leading up to Renaissance polyphony.

EARLY POLYPHONIC PRACTICES

Most of the counterpoint composed in the period preceding 1300 falls under the general heading of *organum*, although there are several different

127

types. Many of them use note-against-note parallelism in fourths and/or fifths, sometimes with octave doublings. Thus, the intervals of the fourth and fifth were both considered consonant in this period (along with the unison and octave). The dissonant intervals were thirds and seconds, as well as sevenths and sixths, which occurred when octave doublings were used. In two-voice counterpoint the dissonant intervals appeared near the ends of phrases (sometimes near beginnings) as the fourth or fifth closed to a unison. The earliest organum was strict note-against-note parallelism, but by the time of Guido (c. 1100) the organal voice sometimes sustained a single tone while the other voice or *vox principalis* (usually a chant tune) continued with a series of several tones.

After 1100 this liberalization continued at St. Martial in Limoges and in the polyphony of the Notre Dame School in the music of Leonin and Perotin. Note-against-note style continued in a type of polyphony called *conductus* (occasionally in this style two or three notes occurred against one); but Leonin also composed organum in a free melismatic style which had developed a little earlier at St. Martial (*organum duplum* or *organum purum*). In this style the vox principalis or tenor sustained only a few tones of a chant (perhaps only two or three) for inordinate lengths of time to serve as a *cantus firmus* over which the *vox organalis* wove a florid melodic fabric. Actually, since the tenor really functioned as a pedal point, very little true counterpoint occurred in two-voice melismatic organum. A type of polyphonic work known as *conductus* furnished more contrapuntal interest. An example of the opening of a *conductus* is shown in Figure 67, translated into modern notation.

Figure 67: Beginning of a conductus from the Notre Dame School

The rhythm in this example, as in most music of this time, is based on the medieval rhythmic modes, which, because of the triple background in each metric foot, gives the impression of compound meter. Note that intervals of thirds are quite abundant, but that they never occur at the beginnings or ends of phrases. The phrases all end and begin on perfect fifths. Seconds, when they occur, are never at the beginning of a metric foot, though fourths and thirds are. Note also that the voices cross frequently. From these and other observations of the contrapuntal practices in this work and others like it, the

Figure 68: Perotin, *Viderunt*

analyst can draw certain conclusions about the contrapuntal style of the period. The strongest consonance is the fifth; thirds and fourths are also consonant but are not used at beginnings and endings of phrases; seconds are dissonant. The vertical dimension is of major concern only at the beginnings and endings of phrases, so that, with some restrictions, the voices are free to move horizontally without much regard for vertical (harmonic) considerations. This results in some interesting "accidental" dissonances and practices which would not occur in some later contrapuntal styles.

This general practice continued in the three- and four-part organa composed by Perotin, which were known as *organa tripla* or *organa quadrupla,* depending upon the number of voices. Figure 68 presents the opening of the organum quadruplum *Viderunt* by Perotin. An important innovation is the frequent use of triadic sonorities, although perfect consonances without thirds continued to be the strong consonances with which phrases begin and end. Again the modal rhythm is apparent; but note also Perotin's rudimentary use of canon in the triplum, bars 7-8, answered by the quadruplum, bars 9-10.

In Perotin's works of this type there are essentially two strata—the two or three upper voices with their unified rhythm, and the dronelike tenor. Although triadic sonorities occur, the analyst should not attempt to equate the harmonic style with eighteenth-century harmony. There is no tonal center, as such. Rather, the harmony "hovers" over each sustained tenor tone, some of which continue through as many as a hundred measures of the upper voices. Each of these sections over a tenor tone might be called a harmonic succession, but there is no real modulation as in the common practice period of the eighteenth and nineteenth centuries.

Johannes Grocheo in his treatise *Theoria* (c. 1300) described the medieval motet as a "song composed of several texts, in which two voices at a time are consonant." Franco of Cologne, in his *Ars Cantus Mensurabilis* says essentially the same thing—that the tenor should be written first, then the duplum, and that the third voice should be consonant with either the tenor or the duplum. This caused some incidental dissonances which are a bit startling to ears accustomed to triadic harmony. In approaching any music of this period the analyst should remember that much less attention was given to the vertical dimension than in music of the seventeenth, eighteenth, and nineteenth centuries. The modern way of listening to music harmonically was a phenomenon of the Renaissance. The medieval listener could accept practically any kind of dissonance provided that appropriate consonances occurred periodically in the right places. The consonances in the medieval motet were the perfect fifth and octave, with thirds and sixths acceptable as imperfect consonances. Thus, most medieval motets begin and end with perfect consonances without the third, although a trend toward triadic harmony is very

Figure 69: Motet: *Pucelete-Je Languis-Domino* (HAM). From Archibald T. Davison and Willi Apel, eds; *Historical Anthology of Music: Oriental, Medieval, and Renaissance Music,* published by Harvard University Press. Copyright 1946, 1949 by the President and Fellows of Harvard College. Used by permission.

apparent. Figure 69 shows the opening of a typical thirteenth-century motet. The tenor still moves in equal note values corresponding to the unit of the metric foot, but interesting three-tone sonorities (often sounding rather like twentieth-century quartal sounds) occur at incidental points between the consonant cadences. Note also the rhythmic independence between the two upper voices.

In the period following 1300, rhythmic problems came to the fore and composers began to strive for greater subtlety of rhythmic expression as well as better rhythmic notation. As a result, this is one of the important periods in the history of notation. The increased secularism in the culture of this time led toward greater interest in secular polyphony and more expressive melody writing. As polyphony developed, parallelisms continued to be used, but more often in thirds or sixths than in fifths. Also thirds and sixths were used more often on the strong beats as consonances, although the final sonority continued to be a fifth, octave, or unison.

Greater interest in contrary motion can also be observed in the music of this period, particularly at cadences. One of the most popular cadences of the time is the *Landini cadence* (named after the outstanding fourteenth-century Italian composer, but not invented by him). As illustrated in Figure 70, the essence of this cadence formula is the contrary motion in the outer parts and the characteristic melodic pattern in the top voice.

Figure 70: Landini Cadence

Note that except for the final chord in Figure 70, all of the sonorities are triads. The evolution of triadic harmony owes much to polyphonic practices in medieval England. Medieval polyphony in the British Isles is distinguished from that of the continent by its use of *gymel* and English discant. Gymel is the practice of singing in parallel sixths and thirds, which has existed among the musical folk of Wales for centuries, while English discant is three-voice parallelism in first-inversion triads. Both undoubtedly originated as improvisatory practices in folk music, but their influence can be seen in notated music as early as the fourteenth century. The first examples of true triadic harmony comparable to that of the Renaissance are found in several fifteenth-century English manuscripts. Figure 71 is an example from the fourteenth century. Note that parallel fifths still occur, that not all of the sonorities are triadic, and that open fifths still are found at the beginnings and ends of all phrases. But note the use of contrary motion and the frequency of first-inversion triads moving in parallel motion.

Figure 71: From an English Mass of the Fourteenth Century (HAM 57b). From Archibald T. Davison and Willi Apel, eds., *Historical Anthology of Music: Oriental, Medieval, and Renaissance Music,* published by Harvard University Press. Copyright 1946, 1949 by the President and Fellows of Harvard College. Used by permission.

Figure 72: Burgundian Cadences

On the continent some of the most significant developments in polyphony occurred among the composers of the Burgundian school (notably

Binchois and Dufay). Figure 72 shows two examples of cadences which became popular in Burgundian music. Note that parallel fifths are avoided in both examples, but that parallel fourths seem to be permitted between the upper voices.

In the music of the great fifteenth-century English composer John Dunstable we find the beginning of the polyphonic practices of the Renaissance. He can be viewed as the first truly triadic composer, the one who first utilized consistent procedures of counterpoint and part-writing based on a triadic substructure. This led in turn to the vast body of wonderful polyphonic music in the Renaissance and also made possible the establishment of the tonal system in use from the early baroque to the twentieth century. Figure 73 shows the opening of Dunstable's motet *Sancta Maria*. In addition to the

Figure 73: Dunstable, Motet: *Sancta Maria*

frequent triadic outlines in the voice lines, there is a feeling of triadic harmony throughout. Indeed, the cadence on the syllable "cta" sounds very much like a half cadence in C major. Often his polyphony creates almost the impression of homophonic chords functioning in relation to a tonal center, even though the lines are based on the church modes. One might call him the father of modern part-writing in that he was the first to treat dissonance in relation to meter much as is done in sixteenth-century counterpoint. Also in Dunstable's music the interval of the fourth is treated as a dissonance requiring a resolution, as in the Renaissance.

ANALYSIS OF RENAISSANCE POLYPHONY

There are two basic Renaissance vocal styles, both of which may be used in the course of a single work while retaining clear and separate identities. The first is the typical polyphonic texture, in which the various voices maintain melodic independence with free imitation or free counterpoint to create the effect of great rhythmic and melodic freedom and flux. The second is typified by *familiar style*, in which all of the voices sound the same rhythms at the same time, creating the effect of a series of block chords in homophonic style. The latter style requires no special analytical approaches other than those previously discussed. Here we will be concerned most of all with the true contrapuntal texture of the first style.

It should be remembered in approaching the music of the Renaissance or any earlier period that bar lines did not come into common use until the seventeenth century. Most modern editions of early works have been edited to include bar lines. In Renaissance music the added bar lines correspond to the *tactus*, the fifteenth- and sixteenth-century term for the beat. The tactus functioned to keep the performers together in good ensemble and was used by the composer as a means of organizing consonance and dissonance. That is, certain dissonances such as suspensions were commonly used on the strong beats only, while dissonances such as ascending passing tones might be found only between the beats. Unlike much medieval polyphony, the composer wrote all the parts at the same time, considering consonance and dissonance not only in terms of the bass, but in relation to all the voices. The analyst, in considering the treatment of dissonance in a piece of Renaissance polyphony, should compare the actual use of dissonant tones with the normative contrapuntal procedures of the sixteenth century. These normative procedures (the main subject of sixteenth-century counterpoint courses) are too lengthy to present here, but knowledge and skill in this area are requisites to intelligent analysis of Renaissance polyphony.

Much Renaissance polyphony is constructed in a series of points of imitation, and since the initial imitative section will often overlap the beginning of the second imitative section, the phrase structure is frequently obscured. This is illustrated in Figure 74 by the opening of Palestrina's *Pope Marcellus Mass*. Note that the first tenors are already beginning the second imitative section at the point where the second tenors (followed by the second basses) are making their initial entrance. One of the first analytical steps is to determine the phrase structure in terms of the use of canon or other *obblighi* (Zarlino's term for contrapuntal devices such as inversion, double counterpoint, or canon which at their initial presentation "oblige" the composer to follow a specific course of action as the piece progresses).* To

---

*Gioseffo Zarlino, *The Art of Counterpoint*, trans. Guy Marco and Claude Palisca (New Haven: Yale University Press, 1968).

determine the phrase structure it will be necessary to describe all of the obblighi used by the composer throughout the piece. For example, if one voice imitates another in inversion or augmentation, it will be necessary to determine this in order to analyze the phrase structure. Sections in free counterpoint where obblighi are not used may not have clear-cut phrase structures because of their more or less continuous textures.

One of the important steps in microanalysis is to describe the use of dissonance in some detail, in particular noting where the composer has departed from normative sixteenth-century procedures. For example, it would be quite remarkable to find a suspension on the fourth beat of a measure with its resolution on the first beat of the next. This could furnish material for significant observations about style. The analyst should bear in mind, however, that the normative contrapuntal procedures taught in most sixteenth-century counterpoint courses, though they furnish a frame of reference, by no means represent the style of all Renaissance composers.

One of the striking features of Renaissance polyphony is its rhythm. In this period before the use of bar lines and before the establishment of meter

Figure 74: Palestrina, *Pope Marcellus Mass*

as we know it today, composers created melodic lines with great rhythmic freedom; and the juxtaposition of these lines in canon or free counterpoint is perhaps the most beautiful feature of Renaissance polyphony. Figure 75 presents another excerpt from the *Pope Marcellus Mass* which has been analyzed for its microrhythmic structure. Typical of the melodic style in Renaissance polyphony is the tendency to begin with a fairly long tone and successively decrease the length of the subsequent tones until a point is reached where a fresh long tone is required. In this analysis each such unit is indicated by a bracket so that the tones under each bracket are in descending order according to duration, or are equal in length. Of interest to the style analyst is the variety of the lengths of the microrhythmic units revealed by this analysis, and the very free manner in which a unit in one voice is juxtaposed to the units in other voices. This is the essence of counterpoint, and an analysis like this can furnish material for significant value judgments at the evaluative stage. Not all counterpoint will manifest such rhythmic

Figure 75: Palestrina, *Pope Marcellus Mass*

interest and freedom among the voices, and this is one of the reasons why Palestrina is viewed as a great master of polyphony, while others are not.

In summary, the following procedures may be followed in the analysis of renaissance polyphony: (1) Determine phrase structure and points of imitation, (2) describe *obblighi*, (3) describe treatment of dissonance, and (4) analyze microrhythm. Obviously, other analytical techniques discussed earlier under harmony and melody will also be applicable. The analyst should utilize all procedures which are truly relevant to the music at hand, the objective being to furnish pertinent data for the final stage of analysis.

TONAL COUNTERPOINT

Most of the counterpoint of the period from about 1625 to 1900 falls into the general category of tonal counterpoint. Essentially, this means that the contrapuntal voices are written in terms of triads within a diatonic tonal structure. For many composers this was a restrictive and limiting framework in which to work. One has only to compare a fugue of Handel with one of J. S. Bach to see that the former did not often manage to transcend the restrictions of the diatonic scale in his counterpoint, while the latter did. This is why the basso continuo parts in the Christmas Oratorio are melodically more interesting and exciting to play than those in the *Messiah*. And this is why certain Bach fugues are almost impossible to analyze from the standpoint of diatonic harmony, while those of Handel are quite easy. Functional harmonic progressions are always present or implied in Handel's counterpoint, often at the expense of the free play of the voices, while in Bach the interplay of lines is all-important.

The part-writing procedures of the common practice period form the basis for the normative contrapuntal practices of tonal counterpoint. Since these are widely taught in theory courses, there is no point in reviewing them here. Except for the implications of diatonic harmony and tonal structure, the analysis of tonal counterpoint can be very similar to that of Renaissance polyphony. That is, imitation is a common device, not only in the fugue, but in inventions, organ chorales, and other contrapuntal forms of the eighteenth century. Structures based on a series of points of imitation, however, are less common in the eighteenth century, as composers began to construct longer works based upon fewer melodic ideas. This may be partly the result of the baroque practice of maintaining a single mood throughout an extended movement by repetition of motives—a manifestation of the "doctrine of affections."

Also common in tonal counterpoint, even in the nineteenth century, are obblighi such as inversion, diminution, and augmentation; and the chaconne and passacaglia. Indeed, certain nineteenth-century composers such as

Brahms and Max Reger found great inspiration in the contrapuntal devices of the Renaissance and baroque periods.

Rhythmic analysis of tonal counterpoint is quite different from that of the Renaissance, the reason being that bar lines came into common use in the baroque period and exerted a strong influence throughout the common practice period, even to the present day. In the nineteenth century, composers strove to free themselves from the bar line, a repressive force with which Renaissance composers never had to cope. Renaissance composers were always cognizant of the tactus, but this did not drastically inhibit rhythmic freedom. It simply furnished a means of organization of dissonance and helped in performance. When bar lines came into use, they became a visible and tangible aid in performance and in the notation of scores for multiple voices and instruments. But like the unities of classical tragedy and like the diatonic scale, bar lines were a sure but *restrictive* means of organization. Indeed, the same historical pattern from the seventeenth century to the twentieth can be seen in the evolution of both rhythm and diatonic harmony. That is, both reached a state of crystallization, from which it took nearly 200 years to break free, at about the same time. The increasing chromaticism and more frequent and more distant modulation seen in nineteenth-century harmony found its counterpart in the increasing cross rhythms, syncopations, and complexity of nineteenth-century rhythm.

The term *composite rhythm* can be used to describe the resultant overall rhythmic articulation among all the voices of a contrapuntal texture. The composite rhythm of any polyphonic texture can be notated or graphed by means of a single line of rhythmic notation. In illustration of this, the composite rhythm has been notated below the score for the example in Figure 76.

In the baroque and classical periods most composers treated bar lines with considerable respect. Hemiolas and syncopations were quite common, and occasionally there were even implied polymeters such as the implication of $\frac{3}{2}$ meter over two $\frac{3}{4}$ measures. But most of the rhythmic interest in seventeenth-and eighteenth-century music came from the juxtaposition of two or more different voice lines—from counterpoint. The composite rhythm of the Corelli example in Figure 76 is really rather uninteresting. Eighth notes move incessantly, broken only by sixteenths, so there is little contrast to the metronomic pulse of the meter. The interest in this example is found not in the composite rhythm but in the relationships among the three strata. Note particularly the relationship between the outer parts—the contrary motion and the exchange of rhythmic movement seen in the varying densities. Also of interest is the fact that this is an accompanied fugal exposition in which the two upper parts manifest the typical subject-and-answer relationship above the continuo accompaniment. Fugal movements of this type were quite common in ensemble music of the baroque.

Figure 76: Corelli, Trio Sonata in B Minor, Op. 1, No. 6, Second Movement

There are, however, contrapuntal phenomena to be observed even in music in which there is little or no rhythmic independence among the parts. The baroque chorale harmonization is a case in point. In examining any of the vast numbers of chorales harmonized or composed by church composers of the German baroque, the analyst should be particularly observant of the relationship between the outer parts. J. S. Bach was very careful to maintain a good contrapuntal relationship between the bass and soprano, as illustrated in Figure 77.

Although there is very little rhythmic independence between the outer parts in this example, note the frequent use of contrary motion and the smooth melodic contour of the bass line in juxtaposition to the soprano. At times it appears that the tenor crosses below the bass line, but when the bass line is doubled by bass instruments an octave lower as Bach intended, there is no crossing of voices.

Figure 77: Bach, Chorale from Cantata 83: *Mit Fried und Freud Ich Fahr Dahin*

The Brahms example in figure 78 illustrates another type of contrapuntal texture in which there is a minimum of rhythmic independence among the parts. From the standpoint of composite rhythm there is virtually nothing happening except the steady flow of eighth notes in $\frac{12}{8}$ time. The contrapuntal interest is found in the contrast of the sustained chorale melody to the flowing stepwise eighth notes moving in thirds or tenths. Brahms' use of the venerable chorale prelude technique is another illustration of his interest in the techniques of earlier periods. Of particular interest to the style analyst

---

*Not really crossed voices, since the bass line would normally have an instrumental doubling one octave lower.

Molto moderato

Figure 78: Brahms, Chorale Prelude: *O Wie Selig Seid Ihr Doch, Ihr Frommen*

are phenomena such as the cross relation (F#—F♮) which occurs in the second beat of the second bar of the excerpt.

Augmentation (lengthening in equal proportion all of the notes of a subject), *diminution* (shortening in equal proportion all of the notes of a subject), and *inversion* (reversing the upward or downward direction of the melodic intervals of a subject) are commonly used in tonal counterpoint, particularly in the fugue, as we have observed. *Stretto* (increasing the frequency of entries in an entry group or exposition over the frequency pattern established in an earlier exposition) is also a commonly used device occurring frequently in the fugues of J. S. Bach. Less common are devices such as retrograde and retrograde inversion. Retrograde, as the name implies, is a horizontal reversal of the tones of a subject so that the last note is first, the first last, and so on. Retrograde inversion is a combination of inversion and retrogression. That is, the subject is first cast in retrograde form and then inverted. These latter devices are found occasionally in medieval music (for example, in some of the isorhythmic motets of Machaut), and in some music composed since the late nineteenth century (for example, the music of Max Reger and much twelve-tone music). Indeed, the four forms of the tone row in twelve-tone music consist of the basic row, its inversion, its retrograde, and its retrograde inversion.

Imitative textures of various kinds as well as free counterpoint are abundant throughout the common practice period, but the single most important type of contrapuntal music in the eighteenth and nineteenth centuries is the fugue. *The essential elements of a fugue were described in some detail in Chapter 4 in the discussion of Figure 41.* Figure 79 presents a fugue of the early eighteenth century with annotated descriptive analysis. In micro-analysis the first step is to analyze the subject itself. In this case its sequential structure, its *tail* or concluding section, and the fact that it begins on the fifth scale degree and ends on the tonic are all worth noting. (Not all fugal subjects have tails—some elide into the entrance of the answering voice without a clean cadence.) It is also worth noting that the tail of the subject is melodically almost identical to the second bar of the countersubject.

At the entrance of the answering voice it should be determined whether or not the fugue has a countersubject (C.S.) That is, does the counterpoint against the answer have a clear identity and does it recur significantly in the course of the fugue? In this case the countersubject is virtually as important thematically as the subject, for it occurs against each entry of the subject and is developed canonically in the episode. Note that harmonic analysis is shown in the annotations in only a few crucial places. It is not necessary to show every implication of harmonic change on every beat. Indeed, such detailed analysis might tend to obscure more important features of the work; and at some points in many fugues, particularly those of Bach, detailed harmonic analysis may not only be pointless but impossible.

Following the entrance of the third voice there is a brief section marked as a *codetta*. This is a conventional term for a section within a fugal exposition which contains no part of an entry of the subject. (It bears little relationship to the term as it is used in the description of sonata form.) It is often found in fugues of three or more voices, usually separating the next-to-the-last entry from the final entry. Its function in the growth process is usually to modulate back to the tonic for the final entry. That is the case in this example, for the modulation from B-flat to F occurs at the beginning of the codetta in prepara-tion for the entrance of the fourth voice in the tonic key. In this case the codetta is based on a false entry of the subject in the same key as the fourth entry which follows it. At the final stage the analyst might find grounds in this situation for a critical judgment. That is, although the false entry contributes to organic unity, it also detracts from the effectiveness of the fourth entry; for at this point one hears the fourth entry as the third of three consecutive subject entries in the same key.

The descriptive observations in the preceding paragraph fall generally into the category of middle-analysis, as would most of the observations leading out of the remaining annotated comments in the example. Macro-analysis of a fugue consists first of all of assessment of the overall pattern of entries of the subject, which in turn bears a strong influence on the shape of the work. In this case the exposition constitutes more than half of the total movement. The episode is also substantial, though somewhat shorter than the

Figure 79: Fischer, Fugue X, from *Ariadne Musica*

exposition, while the final statement is only four measures in duration. Thus, this fugue shows a natural division into three unequal parts. Other fugues have similar patterns, but there are also many fugues cast in distinctly different shapes. In Bach's *Art of Fugue*, for example, the use of obblighi such as augmentation, inversion, and diminution results in many different shapes among the various fugues of the work. Many larger fugues may have entry groups with subject-and-answer relationships (in addition to the exposition) located within the body of the fugue in such a way as to create multisectional effects. In such instances the key centers of the various sections are important in defining the overall tonal structure. Sometimes, instead of a single final statement, there may be a complete entry group with several voices participating in subject-and-answer dialogue, so that the appropriate descriptive term would be "final entry group" rather than "final statement." The essential trait of an entry group is that at least two consecutive subject entries should occur in the proper tonal relationship of tonic and dominant in the secondary key center.

TONAL ANSWERS

The subject of the fugue in Figure 79 is one which calls for a tonal answer. A tonal answer is an answer which is modified according to certain conventions so that one or two of the intervals do not correspond in size to the intervals of the subject. A real answer is an answer in which all of the intervals correspond in size to the original subject. (An answer is considered real even if qualities of intervals are changed—such as a major third changing to a minor third—as long as the class of interval remains the same.)

In the case of the tonal answer in Figure 79, the reason for the alteration seems quite obvious. If the alto had begun on G with a real answer, the entrance would have begun on a dissonance. But there is more to it than that, for the consistency of baroque practice in regard to tonal and real answers suggests that baroque composers were responding to the prevailing attitude toward tonality and functional harmony. Indeed, tonal answers were composed in so consistent a manner that a set of rules or norms can be extrapolated from the body of baroque fugal literature by which one can determine which kinds of subjects require tonal answers and just how an answer should be altered to make it tonal.

There are four basic types of subjects which require tonal answers.* In

---

*A discussion of tonal answers may be found in *The Contrapuntal and Harmonic Techniques of the Eighteenth Century* by A.I. McHose (Appleton-Century, 1947). © 1947. McHose's type categories have been adopted here. Used by permission of Allen Irvine McHose.

the first category are those subjects which modulate from the tonic to conclude in the key of the dominant. If a real answer were used for such a subject, the modulation to the key a fifth above in the second voice would carry the piece into a distant key rather than back to the tonic for a possible third entry. That is, if the subject began in F major and modulated to C, the real answer would conclude in the key of G major rather F, and this is why a tonal answer is required. Figure 80 presents two examples of this type of tonal answer.

Bach, Fugue in G-sharp Minor

Bach, *Herr Jesu Christ, Dich Zu Uns Wend'*

Figure 80

The tonal adjustments (circled in these examples) often take place in the immediate vicinity of the common chord modulation in the subject (to V) and in the answer (back to I). This is certainly not an inviolable rule, however, for in the very first example the adjustment in the answer takes place in the first melodic interval, whereas the modulation in the subject had occurred several tones later. Bach's aim in doing this was to create greater harmonic interest by introducing the tonal contrast of the key of C-sharp minor. Had he followed the more conventional practice the tonal answer would have been as shown in Figure 81.

It can readily be seen that this tonal answer, though it follows the conventional practice of making the tonal adjustment in the area of the common

Figure 81

chord modulation in the subject, is not as satisfactory as Bach's solution. By introducing the secondary key center of C-sharp minor Bach adds harmonic interest and chromatic color, at the same time achieving a more beautiful melodic contour in the answer. Bach may also have been influenced by the baroque convention of giving tonal answers to subjects which begin with the tonic tone followed by the leading tone (to be discussed shortly as category three). In such subjects the initial interval was often changed to a descending third. The second example in Figure 80, however, follows the more conventional practice. Note that in both examples the general contour of the subject is preserved in the tonal answers so that there is no question of its identity with the subject.

A second type of fugal subject which usually is given a tonal answer is a subject which opens with a leap of tonic to dominant or dominant to tonic and which does not modulate to the dominant. In virtually every instance in this category, the tonal answer entails a reversal of the initial leap of a perfect fourth or fifth plus one other tonal adjustment. The most famous example is the subject of J. S. Bach's *Art of Fugue*, which follows the typical practice as shown in Figure 82.

Figure 82: Bach, *Contrapunctus I* from *The Art of Fugue*

Thus, a perfect fifth is answered by a perfect fourth, and a perfect fourth is answered by a perfect fifth. Obviously, it also follows that if the first tone of the subject is the tonic, the first tone of the tonal answer will be the dominant, and vice versa. The second tonal adjustment is not quite so obvious, but in general this adjustment takes place in the vicinity of the common chord modulation to the dominant, just as in type two. Figure 83 is also an example of the second type of tonal answer. Note that this one utilizes only the single tonal adjustment in the first two notes. In almost all instances the answer is predominantly in the key of the dominant with a common chord modulation occurring at the beginning of the answer—I in the home key becoming IV in the key of the dominant.

Figure 83: Pachelbel, Magnificat

A third category of subject which is frequently (but not always) given a tonal answer is one which begins with the tonic tone followed by the leading tone. The usual tonal adjustment is for the initial interval in the answer to be changed to a descending third. If the subject modulates to the dominant as in the first example in Figure 84, no other adjustment is needed. (This subject also fits in category one.) However, if the subject is non-modulating, as in the second example in Figure 84, then it is necessary to make a second tonal adjustment in order to allow the answer to conclude on the dominant tone. That second tonal adjustment has been circled in the example.

Upon observing that the second tonal adjustment in the above example "corrects" the adjustment made in the initial interval, one might logically ask, why did Bach make any tonal adjustment at all? A real answer would have concluded on the dominant tone anyway, so why did he go to the trouble of making two tonal adjustments, the second of which corrects the first?

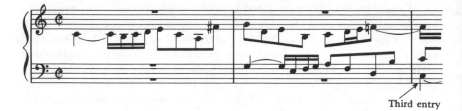

Bach, Fugue in C for Organ

Third entry

Bach, Fugue XIII, *W.T.C.*

Figure 84

Figure 85

The answer to this riddle has to do with the prevailing attitude toward tonality and functional harmony in the eighteenth century. If a real answer had been used it would have appeared as in Figure 85. The main difference between this and the tonal answer which Bach used is that this one does not emphasize the tonic harmony, while Bach's tonal answer does. Indeed, between the two voices, all three tones of the tonic triad are heard at the very beginning of the tonal answer. The tonic then becomes IV in the key of the dominant as the tonal answer modulates. It was exactly this emphasis on the home tonality that eighteen-century ears expected in the relationship between a non-modulating subject and answer. The real answer of Figure 85 would have resulted in an abrupt modulation to the dominant, and the E-sharp so early in the answer would have been most uncharacteristic of eighteenth-century fugal practice. Note that the tonic harmony is preserved throughout the third bar of the second example in Figure 84, whereas with a real answer the tonic harmony would not have been heard at all.

The same reasoning can be applied in one way or another to justify virtually all tonal answers, including those in a fourth category very similar to category two. (Indeed, Figure 83 could fall into category four as well as two.) Fugal subjects in this fourth category are those which begin on the dominant tone, most of which are given tonal answers beginning on the tonic tone. The tonal answer begins in the tonic but modulates immediately to the dominant, where it remains. The tonal adjustment in category four functions in all cases to raise the tonal level by one step. That is, if the initial interval of the subject is an ascending step, then the initial interval of the tonal answer might be an ascending third, as in the first example of Figure 86. If the initial interval of the subject is a descending third, as in the second example of Figure 86, then the initial interval of the tonal answer is a descending second. In both cases the tonal adjustment occurs at the beginning of the tonal answer; and both examples follow the typical practice of raising the tonal level of the answer one step in order to avoid progression to a distant key.

Tonal answers occur not only in fugues but in any type of imitative texture in which the relationship between the initial voice and the imitating voice is that of tonic and dominant. They can be found throughout the

Figure 86

Pergolesi, Stabat Mater, No. 8

Marpurg, Capriccio

instrumental and vocal literature of the baroque and classical periods and even occasionally in the music of the Renaissance as precursors of true tonal counterpoint. In approaching an imitative texture containing a tonal answer, the analyst should try to place himself in the proper historical context—should try to hear as musicians of that time did. Tonal answers can be puzzling, but if one understands the pervasive influence of the fifth relation in the common practice period, one can begin to understand not only why composers used tonal answers, but also how.

COUNTERPOINT IN THE TWENTIETH CENTURY

Many of the analytical approaches discussed thus far can also be applied to twentieth-century counterpoint. As pointed out earlier, twentieth-century composers have continued to use the shapes and technical devices of the past, finding ways to revitalize them and renew them through their own unique means of expression. Contrapuntal skill is just as important to the composer of today as it was to the composers of any period of the past.

Fugues were written in great numbers during the first half of the twentieth century, when neo-classicism was at its height. Other types of imitative textures, some utilizing complex obblighi and free counterpoint, are found throughout the literature of the period. Because of the early twentieth-century reaction against the nineteenth century and against functional harmony, certain composers strove for a linear style of counterpoint in which implications of triadic harmony were conspicuously absent. Often this resulted in a very dissonant style in which it appeared that the composer was totally unconcerned with the harmonic or vertical relationships between the voices of a polyphonic texture.

In the contrapuntal styles of the Renaissance and the common practice period, most dissonances were departed from (and often approached) by step. By the twentieth century all this was changed. In addition to approaching and leaving dissonances in unconventional ways, including wide leaps, the very meaning of consonance and dissonance was drastically altered by twentieth-century music. This allowed composers great freedom in the writing of counterpoint. Without the requirement of correlating the several voices of a polyphonic texture according to conventions of consonance and dissonance in relation to rhythm, composers have been free to utilize all the fugal and canonic devices of the past. In some ways, it has become easier to write counterpoint. This is one of the reasons why complex obblighi derived from scholarly contrapuntal styles of the past are so abundant in the music of our century. But there is more (or perhaps less) to writing beautiful polyphonic textures than simply the composing of cancrizans and augmentations. When it comes right down to it, the ne plus ultra of counterpoint is the composing of good melodies—melodies which combine with each other to form attractive polyphonic webs. The point is that there has been some beautiful counterpoint but also a great deal of meretricious counterpoint composed in this century; the beauty of a polyphonic passage is not necessarily in direct proportion to its degree of scholarly complexity.

Most early twentieth-century composers of any distinction were skilled at counterpoint, for, partially as a result of the neoclassical movement and partly because of the development of the twelve-tone technique, it was a time when contrapuntal textures were held in great esteem. The twelve-tone composers most representative of this were Schoenberg, Berg, and Webern, while, among the others, Stravinsky, Hindemith, and Bartók were preeminent. (Stravinsky did not adopt serial technique until the second half of the century.) The twelve-tone technique, by its very nature, was oriented toward contrapuntal techniques. The fact that the basic row was expected to be used in inversion, retrogression, and retrograde inversion led twelve-tone composers in the direction of complex contrapuntal devices.

Figure 87 presents an illustration of a twelve-tone composer's use of strict twelve-tone technique to produce a *riddle canon* in a tradition dating back to the time of Machaut. Another movement of the work, using the same row shown in this example, was presented in Figure 25 and discussed in Chapter 3. The riddle of Figure 87 is presented in the first two lines of the example, while its answer or *resolutio* is the movement itself. The analyst will soon see that the resolution consists of a statement of the riddle followed by the complete retrograde of the riddle against the riddle itself. The time-honored term for the technique is *canon cancrizans* or crab canon. The use of the technique makes the movement fall naturally into a two-part form, of which the second part is a kind of variation of the first.

Figure 87: Dallapiccola, *Quaderno Musicale di Annalibera* © Copyright 1953 by Edizioni Suvini Zerboni S.p.A., Corso Europa 5/7, Milano Italy. Used by permission of Boosey & Hawkes, Inc., Sole Agents.

Basic row for
the complete work:

But to discover the *canon cancrizans* and the two-part form, and even to complete a tone-row analysis constitutes nothing more than several steps in the descriptive stage of analysis of this work. The composite rhythm of this work is much more interesting than that of most works of earlier periods. Note that the symmetry of the bar line is destroyed in a number of places to create a feeling of great rhythmic variability and flux. This is a stylistic trait not only of the music of Dallapiccola, but of much music of the twentieth century. In this and other examples of twentieth-century polyphony, the pattern of the composite rhythm may yield material of use in the evaluative stage. The analyst should also note that Dallapiccola's use of the twelve-tone technique in no way inhibited his use of triadic sonorities, although, because of the serial technique, the sonorities do not possess the conventional relationships of functional harmony. Neverthless, there is an implication of tonal structure on a tonal center of C-flat. (See particularly bars 1, 4, 5, and 8.) Of particular interest in this example are the dynamics and texture—components of the element of sound, which will be dealt with in the next chapter.

Figure 88: Stravinsky, *Symphony of Psalms,* Opening of Second Movement. Copyright 1931 by Edition Russe de Musique; Renewed 1958. Copyright and Renewal assigned to Boosey & Hawkes, Inc. Revised edition Copyright 1948 by Boosey & Hawkes, Inc.

An excellent example of a non-serial work which uses the technique of fugal writing within a tonally conventional framework is the second movement of the *Symphony of Psalms* of Stravinsky. The work is too long to quote here in its entirety. The compositional procedure—the growth process—will be readily apparent to the analyst. Essentially it is a genuine double fugue (not simply a fugue in which the nature of the countersubject suggests thematic duality.) The exposition of the first fugue is presented by woodwind instruments in four voices (oboe, flute, flute, oboe). Its tonality of C minor corresponds to the key signature, and the entrances of the four voices follow the conventions of baroque fugal writing in many highly significant ways. The subject (quoted in Figure 88) is five bars long, the answer is on the dominant, there is a two-bar codetta before the entrance of the third voice on the tonic, and the fourth voice enters on the dominant immediately after the subject is stated by the third voice.

There follows then a six-bar episode in preparation for the exposition of the second fugue. The second fugal exposition, presented by the chorus, is based upon the four-bar subject shown in Figure 89 and is presented concurrently with subject material and counterpoint of the first exposition. The second exposition is in the key of E-flat (also complying with the key signature) and follows exactly the tonic and dominant alternation of the first exposition, even including a two-bar codetta after the second entrance in the altos.

Figure 89: Stravinsky, *Symphony of Psalms,* Excerpt from Second Movement. Copyright 1931 by Edition Russe de Musique; Renewed 1958. Copyright and Renewal assigned to Boosey & Hawkes, Inc. Revised edition Copyright 1948 by Boosey & Hawkes, Inc. Reprinted by permission.

The analyst will have no difficulty discovering and describing these contrapuntal procedures throughout the work, for Stravinsky has utilized his devices and composed his counterpoint with the utmost lucidity. Having achieved this, however, the analyst should consider matters such as rhythmic interest, texture, timbres, the CT factor—how these along with the contrapuntal devices contribute to the growth process and the shape of the movement.

A work which thoroughly explores the use of baroque fugal and contrapuntal procedures translated into a modern idiom is Hindemith's *Ludus*

Tonalis. Composed in 1942, it purports to be a twentieth-century *Well-Tempered Clavier* in that it consists of twelve fugues linked by eleven interludes. The work opens with a Prelude and concludes with a Postlude which is the retrograde inversion of the Prelude. The tonal centers and the subject-and-answer relationships are selected according to Hindemith's theories of dissonance and tonal relationships in correlation with the overtone series (discussed in Chapter 6).

As our century progressed, it became increasingly clear that rhythmic freedom was a major objective of contemporary composers. Frequent changes of meter, asymmetrical rhythms, and rhythms which were at odds with the meter and bar line were the property of the first half of the century. During the third quarter of the twentieth century the chief rhythmic innovations were frequent passages in which bar lines were discarded altogether, frequent subtle changes of note values to get away from the steady plodding of equal note values, and passages in which note values were indefinite. Random contrapuntal juxtapositions occur frequently in chance music, and many

Figure 90: Carter, Excerpt from *Fantasy.* Copyright Associated Music Publishers. Used by permission.

composers have attempted to create the effect of randomness through meticulously notated passages involving relationships such as slow quintolets superimposed over septolets, as well as polymeters. The dialogue between clarinet and bassoon in the Elliott Carter Fantasy for woodwind quartet (Figure 90) is a rather moderate illustration of contemporary rhythmic practices in contrapuntal passages.

In approaching this passage for microanalysis, it would be most difficult to accurately graph the composite rhythm, and, in a sense, it would be pointless, for the real interest in this passage lies in whatever beauty is to be found in the melodic lines themselves and in their juxtapositions. The composite rhythm is interesting, but because of the wide spacing, the disjunct lines, and the different timbres we tend to hear the two lines discretely. Although they strike our ears simultaneously, they retain a certain separation which is quite unlike the effect of a polyphonic texture held together by the commonalities of a triadic substructure and a regular meter.

The statement attributed to Robert Frost to the effect that writing free verse was like playing tennis with the net down might also apply to some of the polyphony of the twentieth century. Removing the strictures of functional harmony, regular meters, and a triadic substructure may have made it easier to slap two or more lines together which ostensibly make music. But, just as playing tennis with the net down might result in the invention of a new game, so contemporary polyphonic practices have led composers to give a new kind of consideration to the element of sound in music. This may very well be the reason why today's composers are increasingly turning their attention to the expressive potential of timbre, texture, and dynamics. It is this—the element of sound—to which we shall next turn our attention.

SUGGESTED ASSIGNMENTS

1. Analyze a *clausula* of Perotin for consonance and dissonance, bearing in mind the contrapuntal conventions of the twelfth and thirteenth centuries. Attempt to plot a CT profile.

2. Diagram the harmonic "successions" in Perotin's *Viderunt* or another organum quadruplum or triplum.

3. Examine a Dunstable motet such as *Sancta Maria*, observing the treatment of dissonance, particularly the harmonic interval of the fourth.

4. Review the normative procedures of sixteenth-century counterpoint.

5. Diagram the phrase structure and points of imitation in a Renaissance madrigal.

6. Find and discuss the obblighi in an appropriate Renaissance work such as the Ockeghem *Missa Prolationem,* one of the *L'Homme Armé* masses, or a Palestrina *Agnus Dei.*

7. Describe the treatment of dissonance in a Gesualdo madrigal.

8. Analyze the microrhythm in a motet of Lassus.

9. Compare the basso continuo lines in a movement from the Bach *Christmas Oratorio* and Handel's *Messiah.*

10. Illustrate the evolution of rhythmic practices from the seventeenth century to the present using representative examples of rhythms throughout the period.

11. Find several examples of accompanied fugues in the instrumental literature of the baroque period.

12. Plot the composite rhythms of examples of counterpoint from the eighteenth, nineteenth, and twentieth centuries. Note their differences and discuss in terms of style.

13. Find examples of hemiola, syncopation, and implied polymeters in the music of the eighteenth century.

14. Perform a complete descriptive analysis of a baroque fugue, using the discussion of Figure 79 as a model.

15. Find and discuss examples of the four types of tonal answers.

16. Perform a descriptive analysis of another movement (other than the two previously discussed) of Dallapiccola's *Quaderno Musicale di Annalibera.*

17. Perform a descriptive analysis of the second movement of Stravinsky's *Symphony of Psalms.*

18. Perform a descriptive analysis of a movement from Hindemith's *Ludus Tonalis.*

19. Attempt to notate the composite rhythm of a contrapuntal passage of a contemporary work similar in style to the Carter excerpt in Figure 90.

8

The Element of Sound

Whenever a tone is sung by a voice or sounded on an instrument, a timbre is produced, and because that tone must have a certain loudness, or gradation thereof, dynamics are also utilized. Two or more voices or instruments sounding together produce a texture. It is these three ubiquitous factors—timbre, dynamics, and texture—which make up the element of sound.* In this chapter they are being considered for their own uniquely expressive powers in music.

Timbre or tone color is that aspect of a given tone which makes its source identifiable to a listener. That is, if a flute and an oboe consecutively play the same pitch, we can tell which is which by the difference in tone color or timbre, just as we can tell two singers apart. *Dynamics* is the musical equivalent of the acoustical term *intensity*. It encompasses all the levels and gradations of loudness and softness to be found in music. Musicians have always been aware of differences in timbre and dynamics, and undoubtedly they have always used them for their expressive powers. But composers have not always indicated them in musical notation; for dynamic markings and scoring for specific instruments both date from as recently as the late Renaissance, and they did not come into general use until the eighteenth century.

Texture has existed since the time when two or more people first tried singing or playing their music together. When a piccolo and a bassoon play a contrapuntal passage together we may speak of the *wide spacing* as a means of describing the texture. When four voices are vertically as close together as possible within a triadic structure, we may describe it as close texture. When the four voices are somewhat more widely spread, it may be described

---

*LaRue (Op. Cit.) describes the three factors of sound with an image of growth from timbres to dynamics to textures and finally to the composite element of sound which he calls "fabric." These distinctions have an *apparent* logic until one tries to actually use them in analysis where one finds that the musical elements are always interdependent.

as open texture. Other measures or indices of the nature of a texture may deal with the number and ranges of voices present, whether they are of definite or indefinite pitch (or a combination of both), the occurrence of doublings on some or all of the voices, the tessitura of the voices involved, the rhythmic density of the voices in relation to each other, whether or not the texture remains consistent, and variations in concentration (closeness of voices) among the various strata of a texture.

From the standpoint of the composer, many aspects of sound are dealt with under the general heading of orchestration or instrumentation. That is, not only timbres, but also dynamics and, to some extent, texture are determined when the composer has reached the stage of final scoring. Although the three factors of sound are always present in any musical fabric, there are features of each which sometimes can be dealt with separately in analysis. The following discussions illustrate this.

TIMBRE

In dealing with timbre as a part of the style of a composer of the past, the analyst must consider the normative uses of timbre during that period as well as the composer's individual inclinations in orchestration, instrumentation, and vocal writing. On the first page of the score of Mozart's "Jupiter" Symphony (Figure 91) there are a number of stylistic features common to the orchestral practices of the classical period as a whole. First among these is the orchestra itself, for Mozart selected an instrumentation which is highly typical of the period—woodwinds in pairs (except for the single flute), a pair of horns and a pair of trumpets comprising the brass section, two kettle drums (on tonic and dominant), and the usual complement of five string parts. Also typical is the fact that the brass are linked to the timpani for rhythmic and harmonic punctuation, rather than being used melodically. (Valves were not used until the nineteenth century.) Many other features of the orchestration throughout the score represent the normative orchestral practices of the classical period—the classical style.

But there are also elements of Mozart's personal style to be observed in the orchestration of the "Jupiter" Symphony. For example, in the final movement the double basses play their own separate contrapuntal part, rather than continuously doubling the cellos an octave lower, as was the usual practice in orchestral music of the baroque and classical periods. For Mozart to have written extensive separate parts for the two is indeed a unique stylistic feature of this work.

Mozart's use of the clarinet as a solo instrument (in the Clarinet Concerto and Quintet and the Symphonies Nos. 39 and 40) is another personal stylistic trait related to timbre. This is one of the ways in which he contrib-

Figure 91: Mozart, Symphony No. 41 ("Jupiter")

uted to the evolution of the symphony orchestra. The gradual metamorphosis of the symphony orchestra can be observed in the orchestral works of
composers from the classical period to the present. Often this took the form
of simply adding an instrument which had not hitherto been present in the
symphony orchestra—for example, the use of the trombone and contra-
bassoon in Beethoven's Fifth Symphony, additional percussion in the Ninth,
or the English horn in the Franck D Minor Symphony. In other instances it
is seen in the increased numbers of certain instruments, such as the use of
ten horns and ten trumpets in the Second Symphony of Gustav Mahler, and
in Hector Berlioz' practice of specifying the number of players required in
each of the string sections in order to balance the increased numbers of winds,
brass, and percussion instruments.

In order to intelligently assess an orchestral composer's style in a given
work or in a body of works, the analyst must be well aware of the history
and evolution of orchestral practices. It should be remembered that, in a
sense, tight control of timbre was not an important element of the craft of

composition prior to the nineteenth century. Obviously tone color exists whenever a tone is played, and no composer of any period could have been unaware of timbral differences among the various instruments and voices. But even as recent a composer as J. S. Bach did not indicate the instrumentation in some of his most significant compositions—for example, *The Art of Fugue, The Well-Tempered Clavier,* and sections of *The Musical Offering.* These are not abstract works or examples of *Augenmusik;* and the existence of the Brandenburg Concertos and certain other highly colorful pieces proves that Bach was capable of writing works in which the instrumentation was successfully specified with considerable precision. Yet the use of carefully calculated timbres for their expressive qualities was not yet an important facet of the art of music.

Thus, even in the baroque period, when instrumental music was flourishing, expressive idiomatic orchestration was a rather new concept. In the concerto grosso the continuo and the strings (*ripieno*) functioned in a more or less stereotyped manner throughout, and this standardization of role for certain groups of instruments was true also of the somewhat more colorful orchestration of the classical period. In Haydn, Mozart, and much of Beethoven the brass and timpani are traditionally linked together for rhythmic and harmonic reinforcement in loud passages, the basses and cellos almost always play a single part, and the woodwinds and upper strings have a standardized role in an orchestra that rarely varied in instrumentation from one composition to another (and then only slightly).

The highly expressive use of timbre and dynamics was a major contribution of the composers of the romantic period. New instruments were added to the orchestra in the nineteenth century and they began to be used in new ways and in different combinations. Valves were added to brass instruments, the double escapement was invented for the piano, and there were other changes and improvements in all types of musical instruments. It was in the nineteenth century that the first textbooks on orchestration were written. There is no doubt that the romantics discovered or rediscovered the expressive powers of sheer sound and opened the way for the remarkable timbral innovations of twentieth-century composers.

During the twentieth century the expansion of the orchestra continued, but this was accompanied by a strong reaction against the excessive, overblown qualities of romanticism, and there were some composers that began to use sound, and particularly the factor of timbre, in very subtle new ways. This can be seen in the three Debussy sonatas of 1915-17 (particularly the one for cello and piano) and in the music of Webern, Stravinsky, and many others. Figure 92, the first page of score from Carter's Etude No. 7 for Woodwind Quartet, presents a remarkable example of a twentieth-century composer concentrating on timbre and dynamics. Since only one pitch is used throughout the movement, the element of pitch actually becomes non-

Figure 92: Carter, Etude No. 7 for Woodwind Quartet. Copyright Associated Music Publishers. Used by permission.

functional as an expressive factor. Rhythm exists, of course, in the pattern of the attacks and releases of the four instruments, but the music relies most of all upon subtle changes of timbre and dynamics.

In approaching this work, the analyst should try to determine how Carter used timbre in the musical growth process to create movement and shape. Obviously, the key to this is found in the manner in which he alternated the instrumental colors. Thus, one important aspect of descriptive analysis is to determine what system can be found in the pattern of shifts from one instrumental combination to another. Was the composer striving for very subtle changes of timbre at some points and more striking contrasts at others? And how did he capitalize upon the similarities as well as the differences in timbre among the four instruments? At the evaluative stage of analysis it would also be appropriate to comment on the success or failure of the experiment of using only one pitch throughout.

The Stravinsky example in Figure 93 offers opportunities for analysis of some very practical aspects of the use of timbre. Note the reinforcement of accents by the trombones and tuba, the bassoons and bass clarinet adding clarity to the lower strings, and the piano glissando which lends to the first bar a feeling of an upward sweep to the A-flat. In the second and third bars the color is dominated by the four-horn unison with incisiveness added by the piano. In analysis of the total work it might be noted that, although this is a partial tutti, the trumpets and upper woodwinds are reserved for their effect in the next phrase.

It sometimes happens that some of the most wondrous timbres are achieved by very simple means. Such is the case for the Mahler example in Figure 94. Although the solo clarinet is in its rather bland middle register (tessitura would be classed as middle), the four accompanying parts are deployed in such a way as to create a magically wistful tone quality. The violas and cellos *con sordini* fully outline the harmony, which is doubled at the unison by the harp, but much of the effectiveness of this passage comes from the clever interplay between the violas and cellos. The final shading is added by the horn D. Texture is closely linked to timbre in this passage, for the effectiveness of the horn comes in large part from the fact that it fills in the vertical space (and hence closes the texture) between the clarinet and the other accompanying instruments.

In assessing the use of timbre in a composer's style, the analyst should consider (1) the choice of instruments or voices, (2) the mixture of instruments or voices, (3) the idiomatic use of the instruments or voices, and (4) the nature and frequency of contrast within the time span of a composition. The first two of these have already been discussed in some detail. In dealing with a composer's ability to utilize the idiomatic capabilities of the various instruments and voices, the analyst should attempt to find answers to the following questions: (a) Are the instruments and voices used in their most

Figure 93: Stravinsky, Symphony in Three Movements. © Associated Music Publishers, Inc., New York, 1946. © assigned B. Schott's Söhne, Mainz, 1968.

effective ranges in terms of their presumed function in the total texture? (b) Are the technical capabilities of the instruments exploited thoroughly and used appropriately in terms of the context of the work and the period in which the work was written? (c) Are there instances of deliberately non-idiomatic writing and, if so, are they justifiable and successful in terms of the

Figure 94: Mahler, Symphony No. 4

musical effect? (A very difficult and non-idiomatic passage might be "successful" and still not be "justifiable" if the same effect could have been more easily achieved by another instrument present in the ensemble.)

Articulation markings also fall under the general heading of idiomatic writing for instruments and voices. Composers vary greatly in their ability to successfully indicate bowings, tonguings, breath marks, and other articulations. Wagner almost entirely avoided the problem of bowings by indicating only his desired phrasings by means of slurs, leaving the bow changes entirely up to the performers. In a sense, this was not a bad idea, for some contemporary composers go too far with their down-bow and up-bow indications. There are many instances where the analyst might make value judgments on the effectiveness of articulation markings.

There are other instances where it may be appropriate to recognize a composer's extension of the idiomatic capabilities of an instrument, voice, or ensemble. Examples might be the eighteenth-century violinist and cellist composers who extended the range of their instruments into the higher positions, the nineteenth-century pianist composers who greatly expanded the technical and expressive capacities of the instrument, Bartók's exploration of innovative string techniques, the use of new orchestral percussion instruments in the early twentieth century, and countless others.

The nature and frequency of timbral contrast within the total time span of a composition is one of the most elusive aspects of style analysis. Ultimately it is much easier to grasp a composer's general orchestral style, the unique aspects of his orchestral treatment in a specific work, or his differing treatment of a specific instrument between one work or body of works and another. For example, in comparing Beethoven's Opus 18 Quartets to the Opus 59's, the analyst can make some very specific statements about instrumental style: the Op. 59 Quartets display greater equality and increased virtuosity among all four parts, and the three lower parts in the Op. 18 Quartets still function at times to accompany the virtuoso first violin. But what can the analyst say about the use of timbral contrast in the total time span of one of the Op. 59 or Op. 18 Quartets? This is more difficult, but it is a challenge that the thorough style analyst must meet.

Figure 95: Beethoven, String Quartet, Op. 18, No. 1

From Exposition

From Exposition

From Recapitulation

For example, in assessing the use of timbral contrast in the first movement of Beethoven's F Major Quartet, Opus 18, No. 1, it would be appropriate (though obvious) to point out that the overall degree of timbral contrast is relatively low—very much in keeping with the string quartet style of the late classical period. In terms of the element of sound, strong contrast is found much more in texture and dynamics than in timbre in the string quartets of this period. Relatively speaking, the simple use of pizzicato would be stylistically unusual in a classical string quartet. Even the mutes were seldom used. It was not until the twentieth century that strongly contrasting timbres began to be used in string quartets—notably in those of Bartók and later composers.

But the fact that the degree of timbral contrast is low does not mean that timbre is an unimportant expressive factor in the F Major Quartet. There are subtle differences in timbre to be heard among the four instruments (even between the two violins of a specific ensemble), and there are significant differences among the various registers of a single instrument. One of the exciting features of Beethoven's use of the opening motive in Opus 18, No. 1 is the manner in which it is tossed back and forth among the various registers—high, middle, and low. Another bit of striking contrast is found in a passage with all of the instruments in their low registers. This passage, as it occurs near the end of the exposition and at the comparable point in the recapitulation, is illustrated in Figure 95.

Actually, this illustration demonstrates not only the use of timbre, but also of texture and dynamics as expressive factors. Note the use of *sforzandi*, and the close texture in contrast to the prevailing open texture throughout the movement. The passage relies on all three factors. It will begin to be clear that the three factors of the element of sound are so often interrelated that only rarely will it be possible to deal with one of them separately from the other two.

Perhaps the closest one can come to dealing with timbre separately is in a work such as the Rimsky-Korsakov *Capriccio Espagnol*, a work for large orchestra which is filled with striking choices of instruments, remarkable combinations of instrumental sounds, innovative idiomatic effects, and an overall use of timbral contrast that makes the work stand out as one of the most instrumentally colorful pieces of music in all the repertoire. In addition, it makes extensive use of instrumental solos, not only for the woodwinds and brass, but also for the large array of percussion instruments, the harp, and the principals of the string sections. In assessing the composer's use of timbre in this work, the analyst might wish to chart the use of timbral contrast by means of a linear graph, showing how the composer has used timbre for unity as well as variety, identifying not only the various degrees of contrast but also the similarities among certain recurring colors.

Timbre may also be an important stylistic element in a composer's treatment of a text in a vocal work. Indeed, even in poetry there are times when it seems that the poet is relying upon the purely sonic qualities of the words, quite apart from their literal meanings or the poetic images that they may evoke. The poetic technique of onomatopoeia is a good example of the overlap between poetry and music. In vocal music, the analyst may look for stylistic techniques such as selecting a particular vowel sound for a prolonged tone in the best register of a specific voice, using consonant sounds percussively, or using unusual vocal techniques such as falsetto, sibilant or "unvoiced" sounds, or unusual vocal glissandi. Ideally, the style analyst should have more than a little understanding of vocal technique in order to judge whether or not a composer's setting of certain words or passages is successful and justifiable in terms of idiomatic considerations. Orff's *Carmina Burana* and Berio's *Hommaggio A Joyce* both capitalize upon the use of the human voice for its timbral capacities. Obviously, any choral work makes use of the techniques of "vocal orchestration," but some composers, particularly in recent times, have made good use of the expressive qualities of the timbres of the words themselves.

DYNAMICS

The factor of dynamics is easier than timbre to handle at the descriptive level, but the analyst must remember that the term includes not only the differences in intensity resulting from written indications such as *p* and *f*, but also those resulting from the actual disposition of voices and instruments within the musical texture. For example, a tutti passage with all of the instruments in their optimum registers will have quite a high intensity level even if the dynamic marking is only *mp*. Indeed, in a work for large ensemble, the instrumentation or orchestration contributes more to contrast in intensity than do the dynamic markings. Since orchestral composers are well aware of the individual dynamic capabilities of the instruments and write their dynamic markings accordingly (for example, indicating *mf* for a trumpet to balance a horn marked *f*), the analyst must train himself to observe *actual dynamic levels* as well as the markings for the individual instruments. He must take into consideration such things as the difference between a *forte* passage for flute in the high shrill register and a *forte* passage for clarinet in the middle, the effect of doublings, and the fact that increasing the rhythmic density tends to increase the dynamic level.

Bearing these things in mind, it is possible to graph the overall dynamic profile of a composition. Sometimes such a graph may be very meaningful at the level of macroanalysis. Often (but not always) an increase in the intensity level will support an increase in overall tension, and thus will correspond to the CT profiles of the other elements at that point. There are at least three areas to consider in assessing a composer's style in terms of his use of dynamics. They are (1) degree of dynamic contrast, (2) nature of dynamic contrast, and (3) frequency of dynamic contrast. The data to assess all of these can usually be extracted from an overall dynamic profile, although it may often be unnecessary to actually graph such a profile.

At the level of macroanalysis, degree of dynamic contrast refers to the overall range of intensity levels. In the music of Tchaikovsky, for example, the range (at least judging from his *ppppp* and *fffff* markings) is extremely wide. In the string music of Corelli and Vivaldi it is relatively narrow. Historical considerations should also enter here, such as the fact that dynamic markings were only beginning to be used commonly in the baroque period, that Beethoven was among the first to use *pp* and *ff*, and that, unlike his classical predecessors, he avoided "mezzo" markings such as *mp* and *mf*. Dynamic range should be judged not only by the markings, but also by the instrumentation, which generally reaches the upper and lower limits of the possible dynamic range of the complete instrumental or vocal ensemble. In micro- and middle-analysis, degree of contrast may be measured by how often the composer uses extreme contrasts spanning perhaps the entire dynamic range of the ensemble, and how often the contrast is relatively slight.

Nature of dynamic contrast is considered most of all at the micro and middle levels of analysis. Do the dynamics shift abruptly from level to level, as in the terrace dynamics of much baroque music? Are the contrasts modi-- fied by frequent diminuendos and crescendos, as in the music of Debussy? Are the crescendos and diminuendos generally long or short? Are there frequent sharp accents and sforzandi, as in the music of Beethoven? How are dynamics used in relation to rhythm and to melody? Is dynamic contrast achieved most of all by the instrumentation, as in the concerto grosso, by the instrumental register, as in some solo works, or by means of dynamic markings? The nature of dynamic contrast can be a very important category of stylistic analysis and is frequently not given sufficient consideration.

Frequency of dynamic contrast is quite easy to assess in a composer's style, provided that the analyst is careful to consider instrumentation as well as the use of dynamic markings. For example, because of the instrumentation in a Corelli concerto grosso, the dynamic contrast is really quite frequent. A small *concertino* group is frequently contrasted to full or partial *tutti* passages. If only dynamic markings were considered in this case, it might appear that there were few dynamic contrasts in the work.

Degree, nature, and frequency of dynamic contrast, taken together, constitute an important category for style analysis. In music from the classical period to the present, a composer's use of dynamic markings is a meaningful index to his understanding of media and the care with which he approaches the scoring process. In all kinds of ensemble music intensity is governed in large part by the deployment of voices within the texture. A composer's awareness of this, manifest in his scoring, indicates the level of his craft.

TEXTURE

In approaching the factor of texture, the analyst should attempt to differentiate between several general textural categories. These have emerged in the course of music history and, though lacking the properties for description of individual styles, they are useful at the macroanalytical level for rough description. Most textures will fit into one or another of these general categories:

Melody and Accompaniment: A single melodic line with a simple chordal accompaniment, most common in the music of the classical and romantic periods. Virtually all folk song and a good deal of art song fall into this category, as well as vast numbers of accompanied instrumental solos.

Homophonic: A texture in which all of the parts have nearly identical (and simultaneous) rhythms. Examples of this category include the chorale literature and most hymns and other vocal arrangements designed for communal singing. The Renaissance familiar style and the medieval conductus also fit this category.

Polyphonic: A texture consisting of two or more different melodic strands between or among which juxtapositions of pitch and rhythm occur. This category has been thoroughly discussed in Chapter 7 under the heading of counterpoint and includes most of the textures discussed therein. It can also include a texture in which the outer voices (soprano and bass) maintain a consistent contrapuntal relationship with chordal harmonies filling the vertical space between. This is most characteristic of the instrumental style of many baroque sonatas.

Obviously, many textures may possess traits of more than one of these categories. For example, many of the chorale harmonizations of J. S. Bach, though clearly homophonic, may also possess the soprano and bass counterpoint mentioned in the last category. An instrumental solo with piano accompaniment may be written in such a way that the melody has a feeling of rhythmic independence, creating sufficient contrapuntal interest to fit the polyphonic category as well as that of melody and accompaniment. In a complex work for large ensemble it is even possible that two or more discrete textures may occur simultaneously, such as a contrapuntal passage in the upper winds against a slow homophonic passage in the strings or brass.

Like all of the factors of musical sound, texture possesses the potential for constant change. There are no accepted traditional terms for the analyst to use to describe the subtle metamorphoses of texture in the course of a piece of music, and because of this, description of texture is one of the most difficult tasks in descriptive analysis. For the Bassett example in Figure 96, the analyst could begin by describing the texture (in terms of the three rough categories) as being polyphonic.

This, or course, does not sufficiently describe the numerous subtle changes in texture to be found in the example. To begin with, the number of voices (or different tones present at any given point) varies from as few as two to as many as eight in the concluding measures. Sometimes the cello is below the piano, sometimes mingled in the middle of several piano tones in close vertical proximity; sometimes the two instruments are widely spaced. As in most polyphonic textures the vertical proximity of the voices fluctuates constantly, but in addition the voices often overlap, and their ranges are extremely wide. The analyst should also note that in the last five bars the texture is gradually filled in until it spans almost the full range of the piano— finally capped by the simultaneous sounding of two tones at the upper and lower extremes of the instrument. The element of sound was uppermost in the composer's mind at this point. As a final gesture, he wanted the combined sounds of the upper and lower extremes of the piano. Were it not for the harmonic factor he might have actually used the AAA and the c^5. Had he done so, however, it would have too strongly suggested an A-minor triad (C and E in the cello and an A in the piano are already present)—a chord selection which, at this point, would have been inconsistent with his style.

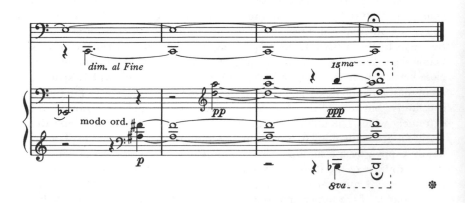

*"Pizz." = plucked with finger. Strings are identified by placing tape on dampers.

Figure 96: Bassett, Music for Cello and Piano, Fourth Movement (Conclusion.) Copyright © 1971 by C.F. Peters Corporation, 373 Park Avenue South, New York 10016. Reprint permission granted by the publisher.

At the macroanalytical level, textures can sometimes be described by means of stylistic terms relating to the appropriate period in music history. For example, in describing the textures of the Bach Cantata No. 140, *Wachet Auf*, the analyst would be communicating something significant about tex-

Figure 97: Paul Hindemith—*Symphony* "Mathis der Maler" (1934). © B. Schott's Soehne, Mainz, 1934; © renewed 1962.

ture if he described the first movement as a series of fugatos in the chorus, each based on a chorale phrase, all accompanied by orchestra, which emerges in ritornello style between the fugatos. The second movement could be described as a secco recitative, the third as a duet aria for soprano and bass with an obbligato *violino piccolo*, the fourth as a chorale variation, the fifth as an accompanied recitative, and the sixth as a four-part chorale harmonization. This outlines the rough textural profile, although more detailed descriptions of texture would be appropriate as each individual movement is analyzed.

Detailed microanalysis of texture may be useful for certain passages in complex works for large ensembles. The Hindemith excerpt in Figure 97, for example, can be separated into several distinct textural strata: (1) the chorale-like passage in the upper and middle brass (the first trumpet carries the melody and functions as the most prominent element of the total texture), (2) the D pedal point in all of the bass instruments, (3) the unison counter melody in the upper woodwinds, and (4) the scale passage in the strings which is ornamented and intensified by the violins playing broken thirds.

Each of these strata could, in turn, be described as to doublings, tessitura, and role in the total texture. It should be noted that among the four strata there are essentially six voice lines, each with its own doublings. An interesting effect is created by the varying overlap of these six parts. At the evaluative stage, judgments can be made regarding balance of the elements, the role and effectiveness of each stratum, and the overall textural effect. Although not all passages containing a mixture of homophonic and polyphonic elements will require such detailed description, it often is helpful to isolate one or two passages to represent a composer's textural style.

THE FACTORS OF SOUND COMBINED

It is clear from the foregoing discussions that only rarely can one or another of the factors of sound be considered separately from the other two. In the Hindemith excerpt just discussed, it should be noted that the factor of dynamics plays an important part in delineating the textural strata. That is, the first and second strata maintain the fortissimo level throughout, while the third and fourth strata decrease their dynamic levels in the first bar to mezzo-forte. Likewise, the factor of timbre is important in that each of the four strata is scored for homogeneous tone qualities. That is, the first stratum consists entirely of brass, the second of bass instruments, the third woodwinds, and the fourth strings. The factors of dynamics and timbre, then, function to clarify the textural factor—for example, to allow the brass chorale passage to emerge as the prime element in the passage.

Significant contrasts or changes in sound, particularly at the broadest level, may often confirm hypotheses concerning shape or form and the growth process. That is, data drawn from analysis of the elements of melody,

Figure 98: Beethoven, Gloria from *Missa Solemnis*

harmony, and rhythm may suggest a specific structural pattern which is confirmed by clear contrast in sound among the sections of the structure. Indeed, contrast in sound is often the most striking factor in the growth process, and the easiest to hear. There are vast numbers of compositions in which this can be illustrated. Figure 98 is an excerpt from the middle of the Gloria of Beethoven's *Missa Solemnis*. Measure 230 is the beginning of the middle section of the movement, and the elements of rhythm, melody, and harmony all suggest that this is an important point of arrival in the growth process of the movement and that an important new section of the structure is beginning. But the most striking feature of the opening of the *Larghetto* is Beethoven's use of the element of sound. Up to this point in the movement the strings have been heard almost constantly, so that their absence and the shift to a closely knit polyphonic texture cast in a timbre of woodwinds and horns has the effect of creating an entirely new mood, strongly confirming the opening of the new section.

Sound may also enhance the listener's perceptions of thematic repetitions or other phenomena pertaining to form. In symphonies of the classical period, for example, the recapitulation is often cast in the same orchestral setting used at the beginning of the exposition. Other sections of the form may correspond in the same way, so that the structure of the sonata form is reinforced for the listener by means of the element of sound. The same principle can be seen in operation in other types of structural stereotypes in music throughout the common practice period. The extent to which a composer departs from or follows this practice can be a significant aspect of his personal style.

In much twentieth-century music sound has begun to function as an expressive element equal to or in some cases more important than the other elements of music. One of the earliest and most influential among the twentieth century composers who concentrated on sound is Anton Webern. An excerpt from his *Six Pieces for Orchestra* is shown in Figure 99. One procedure the analyst can use in approaching a score such as this one is to catalog the spectrum of sounds used in the work. The list of sounds used by Webern in the string section, for example, would include sul ponticello, con sordino, con sordino sul ponticello, bow tremolando, cross string tremolando, glissandi, soli, etc. It will also be found that certain unique timbres are invariably used within certain stylized contexts of subtle intensity levels, the dynamic markings notated with great care.

Texture is more difficult to categorize, and the analyst will find that this is one of the most important style categories in Webern's music. The analyst can use the rough categories described earlier, but often they do not sufficiently describe the composer's use of sound. For example, the passage in bars six, seven, and eight of the movement (Figure 99) can be described as melody and accompaniment; but this does not begin to describe the

Figure 99: Anton Webern—*Six Pieces for Orchestra,* Op. 6 (1928 version); Second Movement. Copyright © 1956 by Universal Edition A. G., Wein.

179

unique sound that is heard in this passage, for the end musical result is a combination of timbre and dynamics as well as texture. Every composer develops "habits" of sound, however, and even in Webern's music the analyst can find discrete passages which are similar in sound. From these can be extrapolated general categories of sound which are not only useful in describing Webern's music, but are also very revealing in regard to his style.

The element of sound is perhaps more difficult to deal with than any other category in style analysis. For one thing, the historical overemphasis upon the analysis of harmony and form has caused a neglect of the element of sound. The result is that, although we have an elaborate array of terms and analytical methods for melody, harmony, rhythm, and form, a codified body of knowledge for the analysis of sound is virtually nonexistent. Of course, this is partly due to the fact that, because of its ephemeral quality and infinite variety, sound is difficult to grasp—sometimes impossible to articulate in terms of clear-cut concepts. Nevertheless, the creative, thorough-going analyst must meet the challenge and find new ways to describe sound as a stylistic category, to draw conclusions regarding its place in the composer's overall style, and to demonstrate its role in the listener's experience. The forthcoming Chapter is addressed to that issue.

SUGGESTED ASSIGNMENTS

1. Write an essay outlining the evolution of idiomatic writing for instruments and voices from the Renaissance to the present.

2. Write an essay on the history of dynamic markings.

3. Summarize the orchestral practices common to most classical symphonies.

4. Trace the changes in instrumentation of the symphony orchestra from the classical period to the present.

5. Examine several J. S. Bach compositions in which the instrumentation is not specified, attempting to determine what instrumentation the composer may have had in mind.

6. Examine a twentieth-century composition and show how the composer used timbre in the growth process and how it contributes to shape and movement.

7. Examine a score of a nineteenth-century orchestral composer, noting the level of his craft in terms of practical details of orchestration such as doublings, tessiture, articulation marks, etc.

8. Select an instrumental passage in which the sound is particularly

attractive to you, and attempt to explain how the composer achieved that beauty of sound.

9. Choose a composer with whose music you are well acquainted and assess his use of timbre according to the four categories outlined on page 165.

10. Select a twentieth-century vocal work which uses the sound of the words themselves as an expressive element, and attempt a descriptive analysis for sound.

11. Graph the overall dynamics profile of a short nineteenth-century orchestral movement. Describe the degree, nature, and frequency of dynamic contrast in the work.

12. For a brief twentieth-century choral work, indicate where the intensity levels are the result of dynamic markings and where they are primarily attributable to tessiture, doublings, density, etc.

13. Find several examples of the three general categories of texture.

14. Select a baroque opera and roughly describe the texture of each movement according to conventionally used style terms applicable to the baroque period.

15. Analyze the textural strata of a late romantic work for large orchestra, using the analysis of Figure 97 as a model.

16. For an early nineteenth-century symphony, show how sound enhances the listener's perception of the shape of the work.

17. Examine the *Six Pieces for Orchestra*, Op. 6, of Webern (or a similar work), attempting to find instances of two or more passages with similar textures.

An Approach to Musical
Sound in Analysis

In the preceding chapter we began to see that sound, among all of the musical elements, is at once the most elusive in musical textures and the most neglected in analytical systems. Harmony, generally receptive to neat conceptualization, has been much more thoroughly dealt with; and theorists have also given considerable attention to rhythm and melody, particularly in this century. But sound, the very fabric of music, is disregarded by most theorists and continues to be the wrongfully exclusive domain of physicists and acousticians. In this final quarter of the twentieth century it is apparent that the relative importance of sound in music has been steadily increasing since the end of the Renaissance. In much of today's music we have reached the point where it is the dominant element.

It would seem then that groundbreaking efforts to analyze sound from a musical standpoint would be at the top of the list for new research in theory. Yet only a few have attempted it. Cogan and Escot* have approached sound from an acoustical viewpoint; and Erickson† has described the manner in which sound (primarily the factor of timbre) contributes to musical structure. The purpose of this Chapter is to expand our understanding of sound in music by specifically outlining an approach (albeit an experimental one) to the analysis of musical sound. Segments of several classical works will be discussed; and I will present an analysis for sound of George Crumb's *Night of the Four Moons,* second movement, *Cuando sale la luna . . . ,* 1969, an established work which represents the trend in recent music toward dominance of the element of sound.

---

*Robert D. Cogan and Pozzi Escot, *Sonic Design: The Nature of Sound and Music* (Englewood Cliffs, N.J.: Prentice-Hall, 1976)

†Robert Erickson, *Sound Structure in Music* (Berkeley: University of California Press, 1975)

Certain aspects of the approach, particularly the graphs, have ramifications for computer applications; while others may be receptive to a structuralist approach. A preliminary step in the approach is to furnish background material relating sound to the specified group of instruments and/or voices. That is, the musical medium as disclosed on the first page of the score can reveal much about the composer's use of sound. Referring back to Figure 91, the first page of a symphony such as that of Mozart's "Jupiter" defines a medium typical of the period: woodwinds in pairs except for the single flute, horns and trumpets in pairs linked to the tympani on V and I for dynamic punctuation, and the usual complement of five string parts with basses and celli doubled in octaves. In this case the medium conveys the message that this, to all surface appearances as far as sound goes, is a typical classical symphony. Of course, that observation will be refuted as the analyst proceeds; for among other things, this is one of the first symphonies in which the basses have a distinctly different contrapuntal part from the celli in substantial portions of the work.

Similarly, the first page of each movement of the Bach Cantata No. 140, *Wachet Auf,* categorizes the textural and timbral style of the movement according to baroque practice. The first is a series of choral fugati set against a ritornello background, the second a secco recitative, the third a duet aria with *violino piccolo* obbligato, the fourth a chorale variation, the fifth an accompanied recitative, while the sixth and final movement is a four part chorale harmonization. These are useful descriptive terms for normative baroque practices in regard to sound; but the analyst must remember that they are "portmanteau" terms only, and do not describe unique stylistic traits. The term "secco recitative," for example, says nothing more than the fact that a single voice is singing in free speech rhythm against a chordal accompaniment of a keyboard instrument and a bass instrument. This surface information constitutes a kind of "cursory macroanalysis" for sound prior to undertaking a more detailed microanalysis.

INDICES OF SOUND

But the true first stage in the analytical process is the descriptive analysis. For sound, this consists of drafting an index for each of the three factors of sound as used in the work being examined. For the timbral factor, this is a listing of the instrumental and vocal colors used in the course of the work—the composer's pallette, as it were. More than simply a listing of the forces used, it should also cite unique mixtures and doublings, as well as special idiomatic effects. Since spacing, octave doublings, and tessiture affect timbre, the timbre index inevitably overlaps that of texture.

Next the analyst might undertake to produce a dynamics index. This may contain notated dynamics with traditional symbols and terms, but its more important entries are those functions of intensity which are controlled by the number of instruments and voices assigned to a specific voice line, tessiture and spacing, and the dynamics of density. For example, it may become apparent here that the French horn dominates a particular orchestral texture, not so much because it is marked *forte*, but because it is playing in its highest register (i.e.: the high tessitura is a more significant dynamics factor than the notated f).

As a test of the efficacy of graphs to be used in the dynamics index, I examined comparable segments of twelve works of the classical period, all very similar in their use of sound and in their general style. The "working hypothesis" is that the graphs will show unique stylistic differences in spite of the apparent homogeneity of style. If they show distinctly unique configurations among twelve stylistically homogenuous and highly comparable segments chosen from the works of two very similar and contemporaneous composers, then the graphs would mean something. That is, they would show stylistic differences in the use of dynamics among the different works of a single composer as well as differences in style between two composers of the same period writing in closely corresponding styles.

The segments chosen are the first sections of the minuets of six Haydn string quartets, randomly selected except that they representatively span the composer's output from Op. 20 to Op. 76; and the first sections of the minuets and scherzos of the six Op. 18 quartets of Beethoven. A representative span of Beethoven's quartets was avoided since the Op. 18 quartets are his only quartets which are unequivocally classical in style, and thus are more closely comparable to those of Haydn. The early quartets of Haydn (prior to Op. 20) were avoided because they patently lack the maturity of the later quartets or those of Beethoven, and thus would be useless for comparison. Minuets and scherzos were selected because, according to eighteenth century conventions, they follow a stereotyped structural plan, are always in ¾ meter, generally differ only slightly in style (somewhat less true of scherzos), and (except for the factors of sound under consideration here) are distinguished one from another primarily by the melodic material itself.

Figure 100, the graphs for Haydn's Op. 76, No. 1 (third movement, first section), illustrates the types of graphs drafted for each of the twelve works.

"A. Dynamics of Texture" shows the number of voices present at any given point in the ten bar segment. (Five and six voices are found when double stops are utilized.) "B. Dynamics of Density" is a composite rhythm graph showing changes in the frequency of articulation of any textural tone. It is relevant because intensity grows in direct proportion to the frequency of articulated (i.e., attacked) tones. The following table shows the meaning of the scale of 0 to 6 on the Y axis for Graph B:

6 = no articulations less frequent than ♫

5 = two or more articulations ranging in frequency from ♩♩ to (but not including) ♫

4 = two or more articulations ranging in freqency from ♩ ♩ to (but not including) ♫

3 = two or more articulations ranging in frequency from ♩. ♩. to (but not including) ♩ ♩

2 = two or more articulations ranging in frequency from ♩ ♩ to (but not including) ♩. ♩.

1 = two or more articulations ranging in frequency from ♩. ♩. to (but not including) ♩ ♩

0 = two or more articulations less frequent than ♩. ♩.

"C. Pitch Profile of Outer Parts" pertains to tessiture in the highest and lowest instruments at any given point, and spacing between the outer parts. Both are functions of dynamics. "D. Notated Dynamics" are included for comparison.

In examining Figure 100, the most remarkable feature is the striking high point at bar 8 in all of the graphs. Haydn did five things at once to increase the intensity at bar 8. He (1) added double stops in two of the instruments, (2) increased the density (to eighth notes in contrast to the prevailing quarter note motion), (3) carried the first violin tessitura to its highest point in the segment, (4) utilized the widest vertical spacing found in the segment, and (5) raised the notated dynamic level to *ff*. All five of these phenomena are seen in the graphs. Examination of the score (Figure 101) will reveal that he also made use of open strings (technically mandated in the cello part), and carefully calculated the tessitura of the inner voices, both of which add even more to the intensity level at bar 8.

What he did not do was to indicate a crescendo to the fortissimo, nor a diminuendo from the fortissimo to the cadence at bar 10.

III

Menuetto
Presto

Figure 101: Haydn, Op. 76, No. 1 (excerpt).

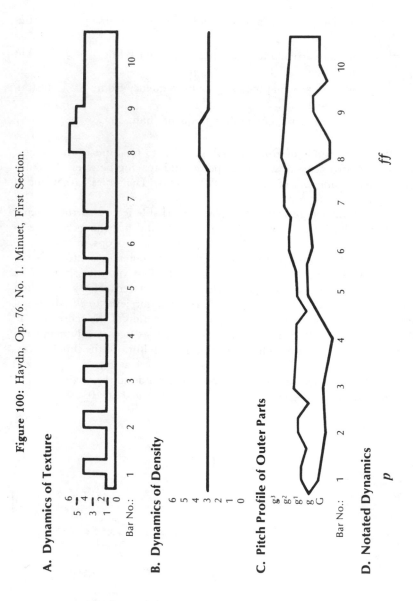

Figure 100: Haydn, Op. 76. No. 1. Minuet, First Section.

A. **Dynamics of Texture**

B. **Dynamics of Density**

C. **Pitch Profile of Outer Parts**

D. **Notated Dynamics**

Apparently a subito fortissimo was desired. Yet to achieve it in an absolute sense would require the players to avoid the natural tendency of the rising lines from the beginning to bar 8 (Graph C, Figure 100) and the increase in the dynamics of texture from bar 6 to bar 8 (Graph A, Figure 100). To scrupulously shun these tendencies is not the most musical thing to do. In fact, the effectiveness of the subito fortissimo is in no way diminished by a slight natural crescendo (perhaps to *mp*) from bar 6 to bar 8, perhaps even earlier; as well as a slight decrescendo (within *ff*) from bar 9 to 10 indicated by the descending melodic line and the full cadence. Indeed, as shown by the graphs, these nuances are intrinsic to the texture.

Referring to Figure 102, it is of interest in stylistic comparison to note that the six dynamics of texture graphs show strikingly irregular configurations indicating frequent variations in the number of voices present; while the comparable graphs for the Beethoven works (with the one exception of Op. 18, No. 2) are much smoother and regular, showing few changes in the number of voices present. Dynamics of density (Figure 103) seems to be more varied in the Haydn minuets, indicating somewhat greater rhythmic variety and the concomitant dynamic fluctuation. Beethoven's pitch profiles of outer parts (Figure 104) seem to be more purposeful, for the most part, than those of Haydn, moving to calculated high and low points, and with interesting variations in textural spread.

Perhaps the most remarkable set of configurations among the Beethoven graphs are those for Op. 18, No. 2 shown in Figure 105. The dynamics of texture are much more varied than any of the other Beethoven examples, and even different from the generally varied dynamics of texture in the Haydn examples. The pitch profile of outer parts is also unique among the six Beethoven segments; and the dynamics of density is more interesting and varied than any of the other Beethoven examples. Perhaps because of the great fluctuation among these three functional agents of dynamics, Beethoven used only one dynamic marking, single *p* at the beginning. That is, notational indications of dynamic change appear not to have been necessary because dynamic changes result inevitably from the manner in which texture is manipulated.

Interesting speculations on the interrelationships of all of the musical elements are suggested by this phenomenon—how one element or factor may, in a sense, relinquish its importance to allow another to take over. Present day theorists, with their preoccupation with pitch, may ignore the fact that in a given passage, the element of texture or that of rhythm, may be contributing more to the musical effect than the element of harmony.

It is evident that graphs of these types can be of use in the study of musical sound in style analysis. They furnish a ready index of comparative dynamics, and are also useful in the examination of texture, further evidence that the factors of sound constantly overlap. A caveat regarding the proliferation of such graphs is the fact that the actual score is already a very effectual

Figure 102: Dynamics of Texture Graphs.

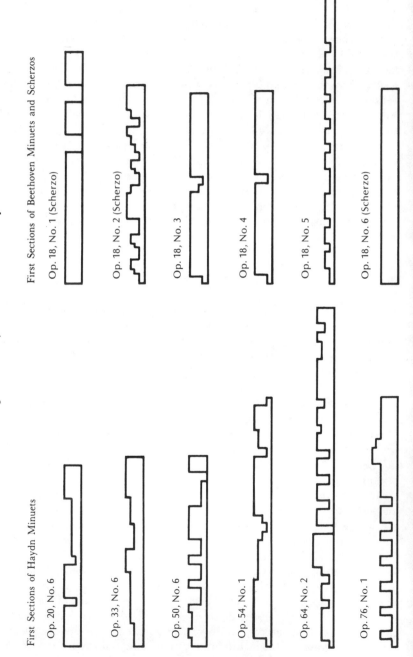

First Sections of Haydn Minuets

Op. 20, No. 6

Op. 33, No. 6

Op. 50, No. 6

Op. 54, No. 1

Op. 64, No. 2

Op. 76, No. 1

First Sections of Beethoven Minuets and Scherzos

Op. 18, No. 1 (Scherzo)

Op. 18, No. 2 (Scherzo)

Op. 18, No. 3

Op. 18, No. 4

Op. 18, No. 5

Op. 18, No. 6 (Scherzo)

Figure 103: Dynamics of Density Graphs.

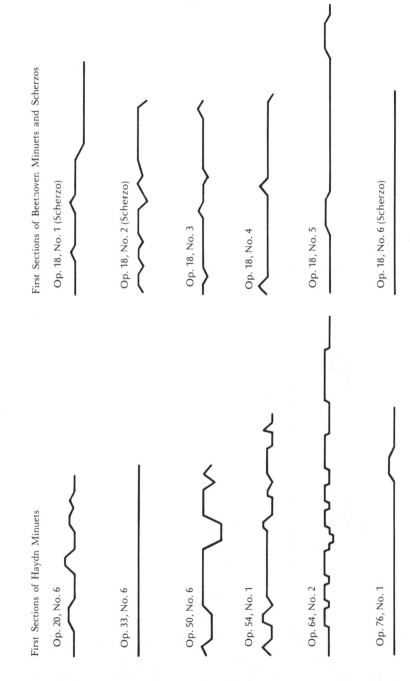

First Sections of Haydn Minuets

Op. 20, No. 6

Op. 33, No. 6

Op. 50, No. 6

Op. 54, No. 1

Op. 64, No. 2

Op. 76, No. 1

First Sections of Beethoven Minuets and Scherzos

Op. 18, No. 1 (Scherzo)

Op. 18, No. 2 (Scherzo)

Op. 18, No. 3

Op. 18, No. 4

Op. 18, No. 5

Op. 18, No. 6 (Scherzo)

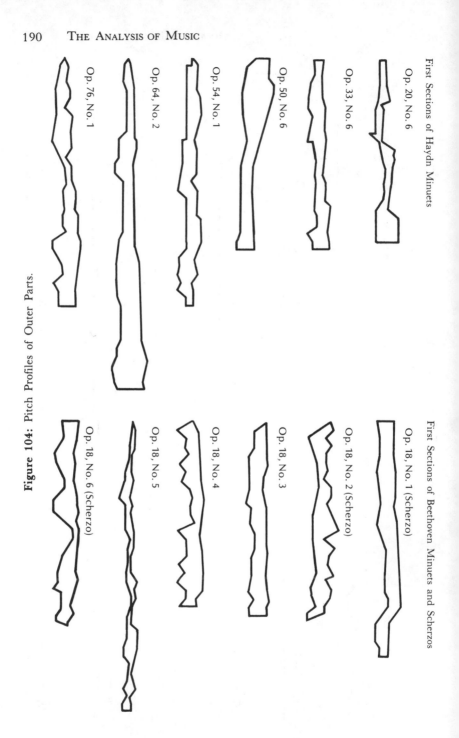

Figure 104: Pitch Profiles of Outer Parts.

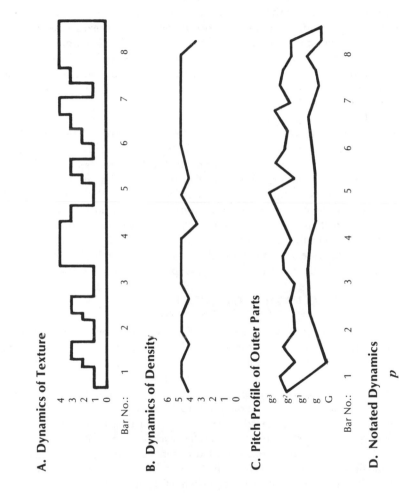

Figure 105: Beethoven, Op. 18, No. 2. Scherzo, First Section.

A. Dynamics of Texture

B. Dynamics of Density

C. Pitch Profile of Outer Parts

D. Notated Dynamics

kind of graph. There is no point in graphing a musical phenomenon that is clearly apparent in the musical notation itself, unless that phenomenon can be better evaluated or compared by seeing it in graph form.

The texture index (and texture is perhaps the most difficult to codify of the three factors of sound) is a catalog of textural information and can be a real challenge to the perception and creativity of the analyst. The graphs used in the dynamics index may also be pertinent to texture. Also, certain specifics of texture can be listed, such as ranges of all voices and instruments, types of textures (i.e., number of voices, which types predominate, etc.), and the width of vertical spacings among the voices. But the elusive subtleties of texture, particularly in twentieth-century music, cannot easily be illustrated by graphs and tables.

In examining a Webern orchestral work, there are no accepted traditional terms to use to describe the metamorphoses of texture. Beyond portmanteau terms like homophonic, polyphonic, melody and accompaniment, soprano-bass polarity, etc.; and textural categories like "fugue" and those mentioned earlier for *Wachet Auf,* the analyst has no terminology for texture. He must build his descriptions out of whole cloth. Yet the analyst can see and hear beyond the limitations of graphs and tables. Thus, each work in which texture is a significant expressive factor (most twentieth-century works) will require its own unique analytical approach, the objective being to describe and evaluate the manner in which the composer has utilized lines and fabrics within a polyphonic web.

EVALUATION OF SOUND

The final evaluative stage of analysis for sound, the synthesis and conclusions, is the pulling together of the three factors in an assessment of the composer's use of sound in the work as viewed stylistically in relation to the other elements in the work, to his other works, to contemporaneous works, and in terms of an historical perspective. Evaluation of one kind or another is, of course, the whole point to all analysis; and there are perhaps two basic stages to the evaluative process: (1) that initial stage in which conclusions are drawn in terms of the work itself and (2) a second stage in which earlier conclusions are used to set the work against a background of music literature and history. In the first stage the data collected earlier are pulled together for conclusions such as, "This is how the composer has used timbre to delineate structure," or "The dynamic markings here are serialized but the actual intensity profile created by certain other factors minimizes the significance of the serialization," or "the many varied textures in this work are organized according to a pattern that reinforces the overall sonata-allegro structure."

Such comments deal with internal matters—the work in and of itself. And this stage can be very useful to musicians preparing the work for

performance. But the second stage sets the work free to be viewed against a background of music literature and history in a broader sense, a stage that should be of greater interest to scholars. Here is where the analyst notes features of the work which may have set precedents for later developments, apparent influences of other works, factors which clearly place the work within a particular school or tradition, how and where it stands in terms of other works by that composer, or why it may be uniquely distinguished or innovative as a work of art.

The sample analysis of *Night of the Four Moons* here presented is not intended to be comprehensive. Only the second movement will be examined and that only from the standpoint of sound. Chatman* has presented a general analysis of sound in the complete work, though not by means of a consistent analytical methodology. (See Figure 106, between pages 194 and 195.)

SAMPLE ANALYSIS FOR SOUND OF A TWENTIETH-CENTURY WORK

The work was composed during the Apollo 11 Flight (July 16–24, 1969) and utilizes several small fragments from the poetry of Federico García Lorca—Crumb has set a number of Lorca's poems. The moon is mentioned in each excerpt and Crumb has pieced them together to form a usable text of four stanzas, each stanza supplying the text for a movement. The first three are each very short while the fourth is a substantial verse of 24 lines. The text of the second movement with translation is given below:

II.	Cuando sale la luna,	II.	When the moon rises,
	el mar cubra la tierra		the sea covers the earth,
	y el corazon se siente		and the heart feels like
	isla en el infinito.		an island in infinity.

It is a multi-media work in the sense that the composer's stage directions and the suggested deployment of performers adds much to its expressive qualities. (Figure 106 shows the score of the movement.) It is scored for alto singer (who plays a bit of percussion, may be dressed as a Spanish cabaret singer, and who sings two distinct roles in the final movement), alto flute doubling on piccolo and declaiming part of the text by means of the "speak flute" technique (whispering over the mouthpiece while fingering given pitches), banjo, electric cello, and percussion. Near the end all but the cellist exit (each striking a glockenspiel plate *ffz* before going out) to form an offstage ensemble playing a berceuse in the style of Mahler against

---

*Stephen Chatman, "George Crumb: 'Night of the Four Moons' The Element of Sound," *Music and Man*, 1 (1974): 215-23.

high frail harmonics played by the cellist onstage. If well staged and performed, the work can have a profoundly magical effect.

Textures are thin, dynamics are very subtle and expressive, and timbres are rich and highly varied throughout the work. Crumb, who is difficult to categorize as a composer, regards composing as a process of improving upon improvisation; and in this score he ably combines "spontaneity with predictable performances."* He is highly experimental in his use of sound and rhythm, less so in harmony and melody.

The three indices given below illustrate the variety of sounds utilized by the five performers, singly and in combination, in the second movement, *Cuando sale la luna . . .*

TIMBRE INDEX

I. Electric Cello
   A. *sul ponticello*
      1. glissando while trilling quarter tone
   B. pizzicato
      1. natural harmonics
II. Singer (alto)
   A. sotto voce
   B. glissandi
   C. "R" trill (flutter tongue)
   D. closed "N"
   E. incisive whisper
   F. unvoiced wind song (quasi whistle)
III. Percussion (one player)
   A. small tam-tam, rapid stroke with nail (by singer)
   B. Chinese prayer stones (unique timbre with five different relative pitch effects, but without definite pitch.)
IV. Alto Flute
   A. pale (non-vibrato)
      1. modo ordinario
      2. harmonics at the twelfth
   B. key clicks with mouth covering mouthpiece to sound an octave and a fourth lower than written
V. Banjo
   A. with fingers
      1. natural harmonics
   B. with metal plectrum
      1. bottleneck technique (string stopped with light metal rod instead of left hand fingers)

---

*Chatman: 223.

      a. glissandi

      b. trills

   2. touching rod to vibrating open string

VI. Mixtures

  A. alto flute, non-vibrato (harmonics and modo ordinario) with banjo harmonics and Chinese prayer stones

  B. alto flute, non-vibrato, with cello harmonics

  C. voice, sotto voce, with alto flute harmonics

  D. voice (glissando, "R" trill, closed "N", incisive whisper) with banjo "bottleneck" glissandi and trills

  E. Alto flute key clicks (with covered mouthpiece) with Chinese prayer stones

DYNAMICS INDEX

I. Copious dynamic markings throughout the score ranging from *pppp* to *ff* with greater emphasis upon the soft and subtle side of the dynamic range. (See the full score in Figure 106).

II. Graphs for dynamics of texture and dynamics of density are shown for each of the four systems in Figure 107. The markings 0 to 6 on the Y axis of the dynamics of density graphs represent relative frequency of articulations from low to high, but are not based upon specific notational rhythmic frequencies as in the Beethoven and Haydn examples used earlier.

TEXTURE INDEX

I. Ranges

  A. alto: b to a flat^2

  B. alto flute: (concert pitch) d^2 to a^2, plus G to d sharp on key clicks with mouthpiece covered

  C. banjo: d^1 to a^2

  D. electric cello: f sharp^1 to d sharp^3

  E. percussion: indefinite pitches only

II. Types of textures

  A. single lines predominate

  B. combinations of two voices (less frequent than single lines)

    1. most frequent among two voice combinations is banjo and alto

    2. medium frequency among two voice combinations

      a. banjo and alto flute

      b. alto and alto flute

      c. alto flute and cello

    3. least frequent among two voice combinations

      a. electric cello and tam-tam nail stroke

      b. alto flute key clicks and Chinese prayer stones

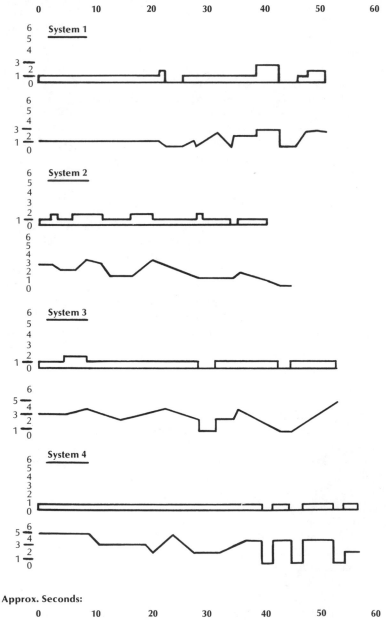

Figure 107: Dynamics of Texture and Dynamics of Density Graphs for George Crumb's NIGHT OF THE FOUR MOONS, Second Movement, *Cuando Sale la Luna.*

C. only three voice combination is Chinese prayer stones with banjo and
    alto flute
III. Spacings of two voice combinations
    A. very close (unisons to P4) with crossing voices
       1. alto flute and banjo, S. (system) 1
       2. cello and banjo, S. 1
       3. alto and banjo, S. 2
       4. alto and banjo, S. 3
    B. medium close (D5 to 8ve)
       1. alto and alto flute, S. 2
       2. banjo and alto flute, S. 2
    C. wide (m9 to 2 8ve's)
       1. alto and alto flute, S. 2
    D. very wide (over two octaves)
       1. none

Examination of the timbre index shows a wide variety of fresh timbres
among all of the performers. The fact that the cello is electrified creates a
new dimension in itself. (Electronic cellos, like guitars, are on the market;
but a contact mike or transducer on a good instrument sounds better. The
composer's specifications allow for either option.) The glissando quarter-
tone trill can be a unique and very rapid ornament if the cellist uses a vibrato
trill, with the anchored finger and the trilling finger pressed firmly together.
Indeed, many high register trills are best played with this technique since
the width of a finger is often too great even for a conventional half step trill
in the high register. It is also easier to glissando with the vibrato trill. The
pizzicato natural harmonics sound rather like harp harmonics and ring
beautifully when electrified.

In this work all of the parts are virtuosic in style, but this is particularly
apparent in the singer's part; for she is called upon in this movement alone
to sing in at least five different timbres in addition to using glissandi and
stroking the tam-tam with a nail. She, of course, is the chief protagonist,
and her mystical drama and virtuosity dominates the work. Her "R" trill
and two instances of written out whole step trills have an affinity with the
frequent banjo trills—an important unifying factor. Similarly, the unvoiced
wind sound with which the movement ends bears a strong resemblance to
the "pale" non-vibrato alto flute harmonics heard earlier. A table of sounds
which have similar affinities can be extrapolated from the timbre index, as
shown on page 198.

This is the only movement in which the Chinese prayer stones are used
and the percussionist plays no other instrument in this movement. Thus,
this unique percussion sound permeates the movement and becomes one of
its distinctive features. A similar phenomenon occurs in the first movement
where the bongos and Chinese temple gong are used exclusively, and the

TABLE OF RELATED SOUNDS

Cello	Singer	Percussion	Alto Flute	Banjo
gliss.	gliss.			gliss.
harmonics	unvoiced wind sound		harmonics	nat. harmonics
trills	"R" trill	rolls on Chinese Prayer St.		trills
		Ch. Prayer Stones	key clicks	
	incisive whisper	Tam-tam stroke with nail		

third which is dominated by the African thumb piano (mbira); but the fourth movement, being much longer, calls for a wide variety of percussion sounds including some which were heard earlier as well as new ones. The affinity of the Chinese prayer stones with the alto flute key clicks (with the mouth covering the mouthpiece to sound an octave and a fourth lower than written) is very striking, particularly since the two sounds are heard in close proximity.

The two most prominent instruments in this movement are the banjo and the alto flute. In particular, the banjo serves as a kind of sound-link or buffer in several instances, its timbre serving as a bridge between other contrasting timbres. An example of this can be seen in system 1 (Figure 106) where the alto flute harmonics are heard first in combination with the Chinese prayer stones and banjo harmonics (the only three part texture in the movement), then with the cello harmonics, and then continuing through the entrance of the singer. This so-called sound-link technique is an important aspect of the style of this movement and perhaps of Crumb's style in general. Its essence is a gradual and often very subtle bending of the timbral spectrum in such a way as to lend organic unity to the element of sound while furnishing variety of color. It is the timbral counterpart of the harmonic technique of modulation.

Although the singer's presence dominates the movement, the banjo player is the most active performer. Indeed, its pallette of timbres is exceeded only by that of the singer. The "bottleneck" technique produces some of the most interesting sounds in the entire work—its quarter-tone trills and upper neighbors bear a strong relationship to the quarter-tone glissando trills played by the cello at the beginning of the movement, thus contributing to the organic unity.

Examining the mixtures identified in VI of the timbre index, one can immediately see the sound-link technique in operation. The smooth transition from mixtures A to B to C is effected by means of the closely related timbres of the cello harmonics with those of the alto flute and banjo. There is also an affinity between the vocal sounds and the banjo sounds (D) while the combination of alto flute key clicks with the Chinese prayer stones (E) is a remarkable combination of related timbres.

A comparison of the abundant notated dynamics in the score with the dynamics of texture graphs (Figure 107) shows exactly the reverse of the phenomenon observed in the Beethoven example of Figure 105. Here, because there is so little dynamic variety generated by texture (as shown by the predominately smooth configurations of the dynamics of texture graphs), the composer relies heavily upon the ability of the performers individually to effect a wide variety of notated dynamic changes. Because notated dynamics depend so strongly upon the immediate human or personal element, the improvisatory qualities of the work are enhanced. It becomes more intimate. The dynamics of density graphs, on the other hand, show constant variation throughout the movement, manifesting great rhythmic variety and freedom as well as complementing the abundant notated dynamic markings.

The ranges of the instruments and voice shown in the texture index are unremarkable except for the fact that the cello and alto flute concentrate on their high registers, completely avoiding their middle and low registers (except for the alto flute key clicks which are below the normal lower limits of the instrument). In examining the work as a whole, it would be important to note that the a flat^2 (in unvoiced wind sound) in the voice part of this movement is the highest note for the voice among all four movements, although there are places in the last movement where the singer might go as high or higher in tones of unspecified pitch. (Crumb in some places has indicated relative but indeterminate pitches above or below a single horizontal line.) The f^2 in system three, however, is the highest conventionally voiced determinate pitch for the alto in the total work.

The fact that single line textures dominate this movement (and are used frequently throughout the work) is a result of the composer's desire to create a mood of intimacy and improvisatory freedom. Even in two-voice textures, which are next in frequency, that freedom has been preserved by means of what the composer Iannis Xenakis has called the "stochastic" approach to composition.* This is manifest in the use of controlled chance relationships which are restrained and regulated to a large extent by the notation, but which are intended to be rendered indeterminate by the performer's interpretation of that notation. The most frequent two voice texture in this movement is that of the banjo and voice, a combination which strengthens the human element through its association with folk music. It is also of interest to note that the least frequent two voice combinations shown in the texture index are those which are most unusual in sound—the

---

*Iannis Xenakis, "La Crise de la Musique Serielle" *Gravesaner Blätter* (1955).

alto flute key clicks with the Chinese prayer stones, and the electric cello with the tam-tam nail stroke.

The texture index shows that the most frequent type of spacing of two voice combinations is "very close," that in which the voices are within a perfect fourth of each other and may even exchange vertical positions. There is a hierarchy to the pattern of spacings, for the next most frequent is "medium close," the least frequent is "wide," and "very wide" vertical spacings are not found at all in this movement. The crossing of voices (between banjo and voice in systems 2 and 3) results in several small harmonic intervals (quarter-tone to whole step) in an intertwining texture which can be said to have been generated by chance but with a certain amount of compositional control (i.e., "stochastically"). Very wide spacings seem to be avoided in other movements as well, so that of the work in general it can be said that close texture predominates.

Moving on from the descriptive* level, let us examine the work in broader and more evaluative terms. From the standpoint of text, the dramatic high point of the movement begins in system 3 with the word "isla" (island), dramatically delineated with an incisive whisper. To my ears that whisper hearkens back to the nail strokes on the small tam-tam just after the introductory cello trill-slides, and this is why the singer rather than the percussionist is directed to perform it. She is the chief protagonist, the declaimer, the evocative agent. There is no other immediate reason for the percussionist not to have played the nail stroke on the tam-tam. The device also draws the eyes of the audience to the singer who is otherwise unoccupied until system 2, and thus serves a dramatic purpose as well. The hissing timbre of "isla" is very close in sound to the tam-tam nail stroke, but the word also evokes its own unique images. An island is lonely, and an island in infinity is even lonelier. The stage whisper, a chilling device even in Victorian melodrama, here is heightened in intensity by its sonic milieu and by the poetic image that the word itself evokes. In keeping with this lunar loneliness, single lines dominate the texture to the end of the movement where it concludes with a frail wind sound blowing on a desolate moonscape.

The intensity level reaches its highest point shortly after the declamation of "isla." This is achieved in large part by the notated dynamics, but tessitura and density play a role as well. The singer moves to the top of her range (f^2 is her highest note in conventional voice, only the wind sound goes higher) with a notated crescendo to f, her highest notated dynamic; and shortly after that the banjo crescendos to ff, the highest notated dynamic in the movement. This is fully supported by the density level as shown by the dynamics of density graphs which hold at the highest levels at the end of system 3 and the beginning of system 4.

---

*Nearly everything up to this point falls into the general category of "description." What follows is "evaluation" and might serve as a model for the topic under discussion in the next Chapter.

Important as it is for the performers to be fully aware of the drama centering around the word "*isla,*" it is also important to be aware of the "sound-link" techniques shown in the Table of Related Sounds. Their effects will be enhanced by the performers' efforts to subtly delineate these relationships. To cite the most obvious example, the cellist on his two pizzicato notes at the end of system 1 should closely emulate the sound of the banjo harmonics heard four seconds earlier. The subtle progress through the timbral spectrum is intrinsic to the changed instrumentation, while the smoothness of timbral change can be enchanced by the performers' efforts. This is perhaps the single most significant feature of the movement—the wide variety of timbres achieved within a homogeneous texture.

The performers must also be aware of the great importance of the many notated dynamics and expression markings. For, unlike the Haydn examples in Figures 100 and 101, and the Beethoven example in Figure 105, the texture provides little reinforcement of the written indications. Fluctuations in density are essential to the dynamic interest and rhythmic vitality, but the relatively smooth contours of the dynamics of texture graphs denote a style that relies heavily upon the performers' effectiveness in bringing the notated dynamics to full realization.

The stochastic aspects of the work are intrinsic to its dramatic effectiveness. Without the element of controlled chance, particularly in the juxtaposition of the two voice textures, much of the improvisatory quality of the work would be lost. The performers can capitalize upon the humane and emotional elements of the work by allowing this improvisatory quality to emerge. The timings and metronome markings should be taken quite literally, but there must be freedom. A great deal will be lost in an overly scrupulous and painstaking reading.

In summation it can be said that the use of sound in this movement is innovative, virtuosic, and musical. It is also representative of American compositional trends of recent years—the inclination toward innovative expansion of sonic resources—to make new sounds.

As a dramatic work it seems to me to be Pierrot-like. The chamber music medium, the lunar references, and the evocation of human frailty suggest something of the *Comedie Française* character—not the expressionistic *Pierrot Lunaire* of Schoenberg, nor quite the whimsical Pierrot of Debussy's cello sonata, nor the madcap Pierrot of Edna St. Vincent Millay's *Aria da Capo,* yet somehow related to all of them. Eclectic and difficult to categorize, its international qualities include elements of modern French and Italian music as well as a distinctly American quality, yet in keeping with the Spanish poetry of Lorca.

RELEVANCE

As stated earlier, this analysis was not intended to be a comprehensive explication of *The Night of the Four Moons,* but a model for the analysis of sound, using only the second movement as a basis. Possibly the approach can be flexibly applied to other works. Not all of the graphs and tables used in the classical works were used in the Crumb work and vice-versa. Nor were they applied in the same way. The separation of sound into the factors of timbre, dynamics, and texture is basic. The three indices, of course, will take different forms for different types of compositions, although most of the graphs presented here will be applicable in some form or other. Also fundamental to the method is the pulling together of the three factors of sound in an evaluation of their functions in relation to the other musical elements in the total work.

At its simplest it is the two step process of description followed by evaluation outlined in Chapters One and Two. Undoubtedly the approach can be refined. It may be receptive to a structuralist approach—to the application of metatheory in a manner similar to that which has been applied to scales.* Whether or not such an approach would be meaningful to performing musicians remains to be seen, though it certainly would be of interest to scholars. Computer techniques are suggested by the graphs; and this could become a significant tool for style analysis, perhaps even for the identification of works of questionable authorship. As sound becomes an increasingly important—even dominating—element in the new music of our time, it is important to find meaningful approaches to its analysis.

One test of the relevance of an analysis is to ask the question, does it furnish information of potential use to performers preparing the work for performance? An analysis that does this has at least some *raison d'être* beyond the circular argument that any examination of human endeavor possesses its own *intrinsic* value. A systematic separation of the components of sound (analysis) followed by a thorough going assessment of their cooperative roles in the esthetic experience (synthesis) can be of real value to performers, provided that it is approached from the musician's point of view rather than the physicist's. It is this latter process of synthesis and evaluation to which we will now turn our attention.†

---

*See "A Structuralist Approach to the Diatonic Scale" by Ramon Fuller, *Journal of Music Theory,* 19 (1975): 182-210.

†In slightly different form this Chapter was presented as a paper for the national meeting of the American Society of University Composers (ASUC) in 1977.

SUGGESTED ASSIGNMENTS

1. Select a brief movement from a very recent work of mixed instrumentation and analyze it for sound using the sample analysis in this Chapter as a model.
2. Read the Fuller article cited in this Chapter and explore the possibility of systematically applying a structuralist approach to the sample analysis in this Chapter or to your own analysis.
3. If you have access to a computer with graphing capabilities attempt to program one or more of the graphs used in this Chapter or graphs from your own analyses.
4. In classroom discussion explore other ways in which computers might be used in any aspect of musical analysis.

10

Synthesis and Conclusions

There is less to say of the final step in analysis than of any other part of the analytical process. Yet the stage of synthesis and conclusions is the most important, for at this point all of the data collected earlier are pulled together and evaluated. This is the prime objective of analysis. Musical insight and creativity are essential here, and the quality of the evaluation depends upon the degree to which the analyst possesses and uses these important traits.

It should be remembered that the various charts, lists, and diagrams which may have been prepared in descriptive analysis are only the means to an end, merely tools for evaluation, never to be viewed as ends in themselves. Indeed, the wise analyst will restrict the use of charts and diagrams, using only those which are truly relevant to a better understanding of the musical style of the composition under study. A pitch profile of a complete fugue, for example, would perhaps be significant if the melodic high and low points were important to its musical meaning, a trait not usual in fugues. If a particular chart or diagram is found to be useless for evaluation, it should be discarded, for only pertinent data should appear in the final analysis.

As discussed in Chapter 1 and reemphasized throughout the book, the total process of analysis can be divided into two basic steps: I. Descriptive analysis, II. Synthesis and Conclusions. Most of the discussion throughout the book has dealt with the stage of descriptive analysis. This is the most time-consuming stage, and it is the stage in which the analytical skills learned in music theory courses come into full play. For many students of music, unfortunately, it becomes the terminal stage of analysis. Properly speaking, this primary stage of analysis should be viewed simply as the process of data collecting.

Of course, one cannot easily avoid drawing certain conclusions during the descriptive stage. Indeed, the process of selecting significant data is in itself a kind of evaluation, for it reflects the stylistic hypotheses that are in the mind of the analyst even before the evaluative stage is reached. For example, if the analyst decides to draft an intensity profile of a work of Beethoven, he is hypothesizing that, because dynamics is an important aspect of Beethoven's style in general, it may also be significant in this particular composition. Similarly, if pitch and density profiles are made of the continuo-bass lines of the recitatives in Bach's Christmas Oratorio, the analyst has made the tentative conclusion that the melodic contour of these bass lines is important to the style of this work or to Bach's style in general.

After collecting all of the relevant technical and theoretical data pertaining to a piece of music, the analyst should evaluate it in relation to the background of the musical work. At this point in the process, he must assess his data objectively in terms of the practices of the time in which the piece of music was composed. Here is where his preliminary background research comes into play.

Let us say, for example, that in the case of the Christmas Oratorio, the analyst hypothesizes that Bach's continuo bass lines in the recitatives are more interesting melodically than those of his contemporaries. To draw such a conclusion it would be necessary to have evidence to support the hypothesis. The most obvious approach would be to compare Bach's recitative bass lines with those of an analogous work by a major contemporary— Handel, for example. The melodic contour of Handel's recitative bass lines may be found to be more disjunct, of lower density, less chromatic, and rhythmically simpler and more symmetrical than those of Bach. It might be logical to conclude from this that Bach's recitative bass lines (at least in the Christmas Oratorio) are melodically more interesting than those of Handel. Then the analyst might go one step further and say on the basis of this evidence that Bach's bass lines in recitatives are better and more beautiful than those of Handel. Such a statement might be daringly controversial because it invokes the analyst's own peculiar set of criteria for beauty in music. Yet without a few reasoned positive statements and meaningful value judgments, the entire analytical process becomes nothing more than a tedious academic exercise. Such statements are among the most useful products of style analysis, but the analyst must be careful not to let them degenerate to the condition of broad generalities. It is one thing to compare the recitative bass lines of Bach and Handel, but quite another thing to say, on the basis of this comparison, that Bach is the greater composer. The last statement is not supported by the evidence and should be taken as a meaningless and possibly false generalization.

This discussion of recitative bass lines compares a small feature of two analogous works. Analogy is one of the important tools of the style analyst. Since most analogies in music grow out of historical, cultural, and even biographical contexts, it is important that the analyst thoroughly explore the background of the work to be analyzed—when and where it was composed and in what musical and cultural climate, for whom it was written, when it was performed, how it was received, whether or not it was extensively revised, which edition is most reliable, how it compares to similar works by the same or other composers, where it falls chronologically in the composer's output, and any other facts that might prove useful at the final evaluative stage.

In analysis of Bartók's String Quartet No. Six, for example, the background stage should provide the information that the work was commissioned by Zoltan Szekely of the Hungarian Quartet, that it was Bartók's last work written in Hungary (completed there in 1939), that it was dedicated to the Kolisch Quartet (which premiered it in 1941 in New York), and that it is published in a reliable edition by Boosey and Hawkes. Other background information leading directly to the evaluative stage would be the fact that the last four of Bartók's six quartets all manifest the Hungarian folk idiom; that many of his greatest works such as *Music for Strings, Percussion and Celeste, Sonata for Two Pianos and Percussion*, the Violin Concerto, and *Concerto for Orchestra* were composed during the ten-year period in which the Sixth String Quartet was composed; and that in much of his music there exists a unique kind of twentieth-century tonal structure.

Bartók's concept of tonal structure could be described in general terms in the preliminary stage and related directly to the Sixth String Quartet in the conclusions. That is, it could be pointed out in the background material that in much of Bartók's music there is a feeling of being "on" rather than "in" a key, that the key center is not achieved by means of dominant-tonic relationships, but that it is used as a kind of focus for departure and return within a fluctuating harmonic context of modality and chromaticism. Other features of his harmonic style should be described, such as his use of quartal sonorities and triads in mixed forms (for example, the major-minor triad with both a major and a minor third).

In his conclusions the analyst should point out exactly how Bartók achieves the tonal center of D and how it functions in the overall tonal structure. Specific sonorities characteristic of the work should be isolated and these should be related to the composer's general style. The analyst might wish to point out that, although Bartók used an arch form in many major works including the Second Piano Concerto, the Violin Concerto, and the Third, Fourth, and Fifth Quartets, in the Sixth Quartet he used a sonata form for the first-movement structure. This might then lead to the conclusion that the work is more conservative than other works composed during his later years. Such a conclusion could be supported by other evidence dealing with the general melodic and harmonic style of the work, as well as by an assessment of his use of the element of sound.

Of particular relevance to Bartók's general style is the fact that, although the four movements of the Sixth Quartet are not bound together by an arch form, the overall unification characteristic of Bartók's style is achieved by other means. The *Mesto* theme played by the viola alone as introduction to the first movement recurs throughout the four movements of the work. It appears in dialogue between the first violin and the cello at the beginning of the second movement, appears in three-voice texture at the beginning of the third, and serves as the principal material for the finale. Further, the melodic material of the two most important tonal areas of the first movement are presented in the middle section of the finale (the finale is in ABA form), evoking a kind of synoptic image of the opening movement —effectively tying the first movement to the last.

For organization, and to avoid the danger of over-generalization in the conclusions, it is often wise to deal with each musical element and the growth process separately, finally drawing things together in a summary. In the case of the Bartók Quartet there is much that can be said of each separate element. Harmony can be dealt with in terms of the evolution of Bartók's harmonic style and its relation to the harmonic styles of the early twentieth century in general. Resorting to analogy, it might be enlightening to compare harmonic usage in his first quartet with his sixth, or the harmonic style in a quartet of a major contemporary with the harmonic style in the sixth quartet.

Melody can also be dealt with by means of analogy, and in Bartók's music it will usually be fruitful to consider also the influence of middle European folk music. This, in turn, begins to draw rhythm into the picture. For example, the trochaic pattern of the initial melody of the second tonal group of the first movement has often been cited as an example of the influence of Hungarian folk music. The folk element can also be seen in the element of sound, for there are string techniques in the second movement which were clearly intended to evoke images of plucked folk instruments. Among the factors of sound, timbre and texture will be found to be most important in the style of this work and in Bartók's music in general.

Proceeding apace, the analyst at the final stage will soon be called upon to make some important judgments regarding style. Generally, regardless of the work under consideration, these judgments will deal with questions such as: (1) Which musical elements contribute most to the "uniqueness" of this piece of music? (2) Is the work different from the other works of this composer, and if so, how? (3) Is the work unique among analogous works of its time in history, and if so, how? (4) Into what category of historical-musical tradition does this work fall? (5) Is it distinctive among the other works in this tradition, and if so, how? (6) Are the growth process and shape of this work unique among other works of this composer or among analogous works?

Again, analogy will be found to be a most useful tool at this point in the evaluative stage. It can be used to provide evidence in support of the answers to all of the above questions. To find analogous works or styles, the analyst must draw upon as broad a knowledge of music literature and history as possible; and it is for this reason that the preliminary background stage is so important.

Directing some of these questions specifically toward the String Quartet Number Six of Bartók, the analyst may decide that the elements of sound and rhythm are preeminent among the special stylistic features of the work. To support this hypothesis in regard to sound, he can cite examples of the use of unusual string techniques to produce interestingly fresh timbres, and the use of surprising textures. The next task, then, is to draw analogies of Bartók's use of the element of sound with that of his contemporaries. Was Bartók an innovator in his use of timbre and texture? Was he a pioneer in the development of new string techniques? Are there other Bartók works which better represent this feature of his style?

At some point, the analyst might conclude that the Sixth Quartet fits very well into the string quartet tradition beginning with Haydn and carried on in the music of Mozart, Beethoven, and Brahms. The medium, shape, growth process, and chamber music style of the work do identify the composer with that important tradition. Additional evidence for this conclusion can be found in the six quartets as a group. Next, the analyst may wish to compare Bartók as a twentieth-century composer of string quartets with the composers mentioned earlier in this paragraph. He may also compare him with other string quartet composers of this century—all of which could lead to some important evaluative statements.

Ideally, if the work under consideration is significant enough, the final summary of an analysis should deal not only with the place of the work in music literature and the composer's place in music history, but also with the meaning of the work in humanistic terms. This is most difficult, for such assessments inevitably will be most subjective. In a vocal work, the text can give important clues to the images or concepts that may have been in the mind of the composer. At some earlier point in the final stage the composer's success or failure in evoking the images of the poetry should have been assessed. It remains, then, for the analyst to determine whether or not the composer's welding of verbal concepts with music produced a significant work of art, and how he realized, interpreted, or transformed the concepts and images of the text. Even in a vocal work, however, there often are purely musical images evoked which arouse esthetic feelings that cannot be conceptualized or necessarily related to the meaning of the text itself. The same can be said of programmatic music.

In an instrumental work without extra-musical allusions the task is even more forbidding; and there are many important works which simply defy such assessment. Yet since the composer is an artist with human feelings to convey in his own beautiful way, the musician should be interested not only in the mode of his communication, but in its substance. Unfortunately most attempts at this kind of evaluation are doomed to failure. Exploration of the humanistic meaning of a work of art is usually best left to the esthetic philosophers. Most musicians must be satisfied with instinctive and wordless feelings as to what a piece of music is really about. Yet these feelings can sometimes be more useful in the interpretation of music than the most detailed of analyses. One of the great qualities of music is its elusiveness—its power to transcend mere words. As Joseph Conrad wrote in the preface of one of his novels, "—the artist appeals to that part of our being which is not dependent on wisdom; to that in us which is a gift and not an acquisition —and, therefore, more permanently enduring."

Index